Our Divinity Revealed

Our Divinity Revealed

Light and Sound Energetic Reality Creates Awareness
of Humanity as Source Energy Individualized

Nancy Clark, Ph.D., MBA

From the author of *Master Plant Teachers*,
Ascendance, and *Divine Essence of Love*

KNOW THYSELF AS DIVINITY

© 2025 Nancy Clark

All rights reserved. No part of this book may be reproduced or transmitted in any form or by any means without written permission of the publisher, except in the case of brief quotations embedded in critical articles, books, and reviews.

This material has been written and published solely for educational purposes. The author and the publisher shall have neither liability nor responsibility to any person or entity with respect to any loss, damage, or injury caused or alleged to be caused directly or indirectly by the information contained in this book.

The intent of the author is only to offer information of a general nature to help the reader in the quest for well-being. In the event the reader uses any of the information in this book of self or others, which is a constitutional right. The author and the publisher assume no responsibility for the actions of the reader.

Published by

Dr. Nancy Clark, Ph.D. Publishing | nancyclarkphd.com

Publisher's Cataloging-in-Publication Data
Clark, Nancy.

Our divinity revealed : light and sound energetic reality creates awareness of humanity as source energy individualized / Nancy Clark, Ph. D., MBA. – Flagler Beach, FL : Dr. Nancy Clark, Ph.D. Publishing, 2023.

p. ; cm.

ISBN13: 978-0-9601187-0-0 (softcover)
978-0-9601187-3-1 (hardcover)

1. Self-actualization (Psychology). 2. Vital force. 3. Soul. I. Title.

BF1045.S44 C53 2023
131--dc23

Second Edition

Project coordination by Jenkins Group, Inc. | www.jenkinsgroupinc.com

Cover design by John Barnett
Printed in the United States of America

*To Divine Source, who goes by thousands of names.
The pathway to you is love.
You dance to the delight in many forms.
Creation is unique expressions of you.
Your Divine Essence is hidden within,
but wise are those who recognize you.
O Beloved, the recognition of Source within
are those who are lost in your love.
We are together everywhere, like the wave and the ocean.*

Contents

Acknowledgments xi

Introduction xiii

Chapter 1: Realize Our Power 1

Chapter 2: Divine Symphony 5

Chapter 3: True Identity as Source Energy 17

Chapter 4: Hidden Truths of Our True Identity 23

Chapter 5: Know Thyself as Divinity 27

Chapter 6: Vibrational States and Frequencies 41

Chapter 7: Spiritual Mastery 53

Chapter 8: Mystics and Esoteric Wisdoms 65

Chapter 9: God Realization 75

Chapter 10: The Higher Self 87

Poetry: Outpouring of Divine Energy 101
        Love Potion 102
        Soul and Beloved 103
        Soul versus Mind 105
        Becoming You 106
        Purification 107
        Next to You 108
        Singing to You 109

Transcended 110
Your Gift 111
Oneness 112
Divine Union 113
Pierce the Veil. 114
Duality. 115
Sacrifice 116
Ocean of Tears 117
Courting with Delight 118
Destiny. 119
Holding Hands. 120
Run Quickly. 121
Late-Night Date. 122
Living Image 123
Sing to the Divine 124
Marked. 126
Union with Sound 127
Wild Ride. 128
Unforgettable 130
Higher Realm. 131
Magnetic Attraction. 132
Being in Love. 133
Love Letter. 134
Wearing Glasses. 135
Love toward You 136
Secret Love Affair 137
Quietness 138
Do You Hear? 139
Conversation 140
Fresh Flowers 142

Contents

Medicine 143
Divine Elixir 144
Heartache 146
Gaia 147
Awakening 148
Pierced My Heart 149
Our Time 150
Awake! 151
Beloved is Waiting 152
Captivity 153
Crazy Love 154
Divine Love Call 155
Grace 156
Heart Sense 157
Drowning 158
Life Changes 159
Love Call 160
Love Has Come 161
Forever Together 162
Love Rays 163

Endnotes 165
About the Author 171

Acknowledgments

I would like to thank Divine Source for this unique expression of life and the ability to serve the Divine Plan. I would like to express my gratitude to all the people who have come into my life who have reminded me of my true identity, without whom this book would not have been possible. So many teachers who all had something to add and cause the remembrance, including the Master Plant Teacher, Mother Ayahuasca. I want to honor so many beautiful souls who have walked along with me, some for a short while and others for much longer. I applaud you, brave souls, for coming into this world to understand more deeply your true identity as a piece of Source by experiencing the illusion of separation.

Introduction

Why do you feel alone?
When have I told you,
you are alone?

This feeling is fleeting,
Comes and goes.
Can't you see me,
next to you,
looking into your eyes?

Beautiful one,
special one,
how can I ever,
forget you?

You are made from,
the essence of myself.

I loved you before,
Heavens were created.

How can I forget myself?

~ *Nancy Clark*

Chapter 1

Realize Our Power

This is the moment to realize our power. We can know with certainty that our power extends far beyond the small sacred planet that holds us. All life is connected, and consciousness is infinite. What does this mean? You are everything. We live in power as we resonate with Vibrational Frequency of Creator Source. We become human to experience the dream and duality, then return to Oneness. Desiring soul experience, we became human. In many moments we may feel alone yet always know we are never alone. Always remember that life is working for us. Love carries us and places us gently on the Path of Truth and Light. We are safe, and this world is not our destination. We are transcending as a beautiful butterfly. When our little cocoon feels dark and hopeless, find the pinpoint of Light and break through! It is here that we remember we can fly!

Let us not underestimate how powerful we are. We need to realize not to look to others to fix any problems. We are creator beings and therefore have the power to make any changes needed in our life. We need to understand the power we have inside of ourselves. What are we going to do with our lives? How can we be a part of the changes that need to come? Be a part of a community of creation toward a new way of living on this planet based on the knowledge of our True Identity. Our life is our contribution to this world. Now is the time to utilize our Divinity toward creating and helping humanity to move forward on this journey of discovery toward exposing this knowledge of how each Soul is made of Pure Source Energy.

It is the Divine Absolute Source that has created all of the seen and unseen realms, all energies, and all frequencies. Source Light flows throughout all of the galaxies and universes. Our planet is one of the many transmitters and receptors of Light and Sound, which also flow through us. We are learning more each day on how to reconnect with our Sacred Source Frequency and how our planet is vibrating faster and how we will recognize that we are this Light and Sound Frequency of Source. Humanity must open its mind and consciousness to receive the elixir from Super Consciousness, the Higher Self, the Soul. It is important to reflect on our relationship with Divinity. Let us remember that Source has many sacred names and forms yet is far above these names and forms. It is the ALL, the Divine Source. We are the Lights of the Great Light. Let us keep our Source Light connection with us as we walk through our days. We are God's Light, Light Ambassadors. Let us light up the Earth, bringing forth love and joy to this world. We need to understand that Earth is a place for the highest degree of soul growth by using chaos and challenges as a catalyst—this provides a broader perspective. Source has longed to see humanity thrive and remember who they are.

When people say it's all an illusion, what they are saying is that everything is energy. The energy has slowed down in order to manifest into physical form. We are both energy and physical form. The quantum field, it's both physical and energetic, which allows for both to exist at the same time. We are Light, we are Sound, we are Energy, and we can manifest into physical form. The Soul incarnates into this earth astronaut suit (a human body), which allows for energy to experience physicality. It all matters; there is a reason why each one of us decided to experience being physical. We are allowed to experience all that the energetic field has to offer us. We learn how to navigate all of these different dimensional fields while we are in this physical reality. We don't want to deny that it's physical, and we also don't want to deny that it's all energy. We are balancing both of these realities. Some people will say it's not real and it does not matter. Well, it all matters. We came here to have this physical reality, and it is just as real.

We are learning to utilize different viewpoints. All of these different dimensional realities: mental, emotional, astral, etheric, physical, energetic, Light and Sound vibrational frequencies, Higher Self, cosmic, the different consciousness levels and ways of beingness, to name a few. This is us holding our multidimensional reality. This is both an illusion and a real physical experience. Let's not step out of this physical reality and deny the reason we came to have this third-dimensional reality of time and space. We have purpose work, and yet it's all an illusion because it's not even physical; it's really energetic. We are definitely in a massively intense physical reality, and we need to honor it—honor the full spectrum of experiences and consciousnesses that we can hold. We are physical, yet we are not physical, for we are energy. Our bodies are made of atomic energy, which consists of the atoms inside of us. Since everything is inside of us, we have access to it all: the ability to learn how to go inside naturally in order to access these different dimensions for healing, to remember who we are, to experience the energetic world, and more. Many ancient belief systems knew of our sacred nature and true identity. They taught these spiritual esoteric wisdoms and have left many books, scrolls, hieroglyphs, stone tablets, and so forth to remind us of our true identity.

This book will show that everything is made of light and sound energy and that this energetic reality can help people come closer to the truth that they are energy individualized, called Souls of Pure Source Energy. Having this awareness helps people awaken to their true identity, which transforms their viewpoint toward life and ultimately brings them closer to the Divine Essence. Recognition that everything is made of energy creates a release from this physical reality, knowing it's just energy at a slower rate that has taken form into physicality. We are Source Energy manifested to experience being in physical form, and this shows Soul's Oneness with God.

Chapter 2

Divine Symphony

The life force of humans is the precious sacred breath. Our breath is a vibrational and frequency movement in the physical form. When there is movement of any kind, there is a vibration, which is a form of sound. Everything in the material world is made up of atoms, which create a vibrational frequency due to the spin of the electron's movement. From the microcosm to the macrocosm, all has a harmonic frequency of Source Frequency. We are Source Energy Frequency in form. There is nothing but Source Energy in harmonic movement. We are a walking Temple of Source. The Higher Self (Soul) is the Divine within us. The transformation is to know one's own true identity as Source in material form.[1] There are different vibrational wave patterns, and the light spectrum is a wave form of different vibrational frequencies, which is the manifested sound.[2] Source has created everything and has a unique vibrational pattern of oscillating energy also referred to as Life Force. This Life Force is known by many names: the Egyptians called it the *Ankh*, the Hindus called it *Prana*, the Chinese called it *Chi*, and in Japan it is called *Ki*. Source is known by many names, yet they all point to the Divine.[3]

The Primortal Sound is from which all things seen and unseen are created. Everything has a unique vibrational frequency, which simulates this reality of objects. Source created this universe with this Primortal Vibration that is the essence of and within all. Humanity is a race of gods, waking up to the truth that Source Essence is not only Within but also IS Source Essence Itself. We are Light and Sound in physical form, a human instrument. This Celestial Music is from Light and Sound frequencies, the Divine Symphony.[4] There are symphonic Sound frequencies that are sacred and provide sustenance from Source. Source's *one song* assists us during our life here while on this planet. We are supported by this constant melodious musical verse and need to anchor our consciousness to the Ultimate Divine Frequency whose vibratory energetics are within us.[5] Source is Energy, and this creates a sound wave of frequencies that radiate out into the universe. Everything manifested and unmanifested has a unique frequency. This musical melody of the Primordial Sound has a creative power to create everything we see and even higher densities beyond the physical senses.[6] We are this majesty of sound from Source, and even though we don't hear the internal melody, every movement is a celebration with the Divine. [7]

We live in a universe made up of sound waveforms, which create music and harmonics. These sound waves create the light spectrum. Sine waves are light, and this reality is made up of these light and sound waves that make up patterns. Each object will be a different pattern. There are different ways of describing this, such as everything is made up of atoms, which create an electromagnetic field since the electrons and protons are moving around the nucleus, which is sound vibrations. Another way of describing this is we live in a world of waveforms, such as sine waves that are sound. There is also music, which is the harmonious sound current, the Divine's symphony.[8] Everything in this universe (One-Verse) is Source Symphonic Vibrational Energy.[9] All of creation serenades the Creator's symphonic sound of magnificence.[10] There is this *sea of energy* that permeates throughout the universe. We can only see with our senses this third-dimensional reality, yet there is an enormous amount of energy throughout the cosmos. There is all this potentiality of energy that exists that is way beyond the physical reality. We are enmeshed in this ocean, and the waves are the loud cosmic concert of vibrational energy, which is the frequencies of Light and Sound. Source is the Concert Master.[11]

All that we see is Source expressing Itself back to Itself.[12] Dr. Paul Masters also shares of our unity with Source, and this is our interior compass that provides positive outcomes while we are in physical form.[13] Divinity is experiencing Itself in all things. Everything delights in this opportunity of unique expression.[14] Source is within all, and all is within Source. It is a mystery that few understand, yet everything is the universe, which operates by this spiritual law.[15] Source created a sound vibration, and the universe was created from its cosmic music. This sound is known by numerous names that have been created and expressed over the many yugas and by various cultures.[16] Source is described as pure energy of an expansive size, filled with an unlimited love toward all aspects of Itself.[17]

The Bible talks about the Word, the Universe, the Voice of God, and the Word of God. The "Music of the Spheres" was mentioned by Pythagoras as hearing God's Voice. God's Word is God's Voice, which is Sound that is the creative power. The human voice is a sacred tool and can raise one's harmonic frequency by the sound that is emitted, which could be from words, songs, mantras, and so forth. Humans have a voice that produces sounds. We can sing and create music with our voice. Source is present within the human form to create sounds and words. Light comes from Sound, so this is how the etheric body, which is the Light Body that is self-luminous, is created and sustained (NIV John 1:1).[18] The "Cosmic Sound" is the Music of the Spheres materialized in the human. The ancients have always claimed how the Word is Source's life-giving Sound to not only create but also sustain the ALL in the ONE Universal Symphony.[19] The oldest literature is the Indian Vedas, and the Rig Veda is the most ancient wisdom and speaks of the word *Nada*, which is translated directly to mean Sound. Another significant word in the Vedas is *nada brahma*, which is the most amazing in that it means God is Sound. The Bible speaks in John 1:1 of the Word, and then we have a Sanskrit word in the Vedas of *Vac*, whose meaning is Word. The Indian sages talk of how this Word has the highest power of creation and comes from Source.[20] Divine Vibration creating everything with Sound is within many ancient cultures. In some texts, the Universal Primortal Sound is stated as the one creative act of Source. Other times, the ancient texts will state that each object, animate or inanimate, was created through the use of the "Word" or "Words," which is a manifestation of vibrational sounds.[21]

Atoms are energy that is in constant vibration, and they move at different levels of sound and light frequencies. We are the Word made flesh due to being in tune with the breath of Source. The human body is made up of atoms, which are pure energy. Atoms are our energetic nature. The human breathes and creates this resonance with the Word.[22] Sound is the foundational energy that creates all the organs, tissues, and everything in the human body, right down to the atoms within each and every cell in the molecular biology. Our atoms sing and vibrate to the musical sound from Source. We are human transformers that send and receive vibrational sound frequencies. We feel the vibrations of other people; we send vibrational sound frequencies out into the world and beyond. When we meet someone or go to a place that is a similar vibrational frequency, we are in what would be called resonance. We are constantly receiving Light and Sound transmissions from Source Frequency.[23]

Sound and vibrational frequencies created the universe and were recognized by the ancients. The Egyptians called them the Word.

Pythagoras called them, and coined the term, *Music of the Spheres*. Hindus referred to them as the vibratory sound that can be sung by the human voice as OM. The Chinese knew of this energy and called it the Life Force, the Chi that creates the harmony of sounds within the body and brings life and sustains life.[24] The Word of God is energy manifested as Light and Sound radiating out manifesting as our life. A student of Qabbalah masters this supreme Word and comes to understand that they are the Word made flesh.[25] Humans are the Word (Divine Sound Essence) made flesh. In John 1:14, it explains how this Word is in each one of us. Source Light and Sound are our True Identity. We are all sparks of light from the Divine Light of Source. We are Lights from the Greater Light.[26]

Egyptian religion taught that the meaning for sound is "voice" and that each human has a musical instrument, which is their personal voice. The Egyptian priests and priestesses knew how important the human's voice was and would safeguard it, only allowing the highest energetic sound frequency to come from their mouth.[27] Elkington mentions a researcher named John Reid who did an acoustic experiment that took place inside the King's Chamber and in other areas inside the Great Pyramid. A sine-wave oscillator was connected to a speaker and used to create vibrational frequencies by observing fine grains of sand forming into images at different sound frequencies. At the different sound frequencies (hertz) the Egyptian hieroglyph images showed up in the grains of sand on the membrane of the oscillator. In sonics, different vibration levels cause sand to form shapes.[28]

The sacred name of Source is imbued into icons and glyphs. Source is all that exists, and there are many forms of the Primortal Sound. Source Light and Sound Energy is the frequency of Pure Love.[29] The "Rays of Creation" are mentioned as the different musical tones of do, re, me, fa, sol, la, ti, do, which are the musical tones that the human voice can sing. The tone of sol correlates to the tone of our local Sun.[30] Seven Musical Tones in the human body create an energy field around the body that affects consciousness and connects us to the true inner Source Frequency. The Egyptians knew how to utilize these Seven Musical Tones and included them with their voice in their spiritual ceremonies.[31] We are enmeshed in the loud cosmic concert of vibrational energy, which is the frequencies of Light and Sound, which has been also called the "Audible Life Stream." Source is the Concert Master, and the soul can enjoy this sustaining harmony of celestial music.[32] Ancient cultures know that all was created by sound frequencies that could be spoken from human vocal cords, which could raise or lower their own unique energetic signature frequency.[33]

Guido of Arrezo, a Benedictine monk (c. 1000 CE), brought forth an old wisdom from an ancient Arabic text of the vocal tones (do, re, mi, fa, sol, la) into usage again. Benedictine monks sing most of the day, so this would have been a true gem of ancient wisdom to enjoy and add into their harmonious chant songs. The Benedictine monk Guido of Arrezo was credited with the musical tones of do, re, mi, fa, sol, la, yet Al-Kindi from ninth-century Babylon was a philosopher who discussed musical theories and most likely tapped into the wisdom of the Ancient Greeks, where music was referenced as Pythagoras' symphony of the spheres.[34] Words are sounds, and music has different vibrational sounds and frequencies. When these seven tones are sung with the human voice, a sacred sound comes forth out of the Human Temple.[35]

There is a vibrational power that creates the universe, and this frequency of music goes out that can be picked up with such a sweet melody that is captivating to the soul: Vibrational Frequency of Light and Sound from Source. Super Consciousness of Source is performing its songs of Sound and Light frequencies. The Divine Conductor of the sound frequency creates a concert.[36] Egyptian hieroglyph images were created with sound inside the Great Pyramid. Mer means pyramid.

The Priestesses known as the Maids of Mer (Mermaids) would sing at different hertz levels, and the fine sand placed inside the pyramid in Egyptian times would create images. The Egyptian symbols, known as hieroglyphs, are a sound-based language. The seven tones are do, re, me, fa, sol, la, ti, which are at different acoustic sound frequencies when sung or played and create different hertz levels. The human body is a musical instrument.[37]

All of life, all of the universe, is composed of vibrational tones that radiate outward to allow for creation. The ancients knew that all is energy and therefore all is a vibratory harmonic symphony that is sung throughout all of creation. It's Source Energy singing to us and letting us know that we are this cosmic music. We are the sound, we are the light, we are the colors, and we are the musical notes just vibrating at different frequencies that create this great fantastic array of music, yet the music makes everything seen and unseen. Vibration, sound, light, frequencies, power, and the Word are all one in the same.[38] Pythagoras is mentioned as having stated that there is a symphonic melody that plays throughout the universe. This melodious music of the spheres that sings out to all can be heard by the soul. The creation is singing to us. There is a correlation with "numerical ratios" and the euphonic musical sounds.[39]

David Elkington mentions a friend named Professor Christine el-Mahdy from the British School of Egyptology. Elkington shares of their conversation regarding the images that occurred in the fine sand on the oscillator, inside the Great Pyramid, during this sound frequency experiment. David Elkington states that both eyes of the Horus images appeared together in the fine sand at a certain sound frequency. The news was so intense that Christine el-Mahdy fainted upon hearing of how both the Left Eye of Horus and the Right Eye of Horus appeared together at the same exact time in the fine sand on the sound oscillator that was placed on top of the sarcophagus. The reason el-Mahdy fainted was this experiment proved a secret truth. In the Egyptian religion it was so well hidden, this esoteric truth of how the Egyptians were Monotheistic, believing in only One God. The demi-gods were just aspects of the whole Infinite Source Frequency. The double symbol of Horus's Left and Right Eyes together was this symbol of the secret esoteric truth that represented the One Infinite True Source. This belief in One God (Source) was so sacred that it was not revealed until the last historical period of Egypt. This was finally revealed as the name *Neb-edjer*, which means Lord of the Infinite. This experiment that John Reid performed in the Great Pyramid proved that the Egyptian religion was indeed Monotheistic. The Egyptians knew of this Infinite Source Energy that manifested as a Soul in physical form. This is why the Egyptians knew how important Soul's life is here in the physical realm. The Afterlife was determined by how a Soul lived their life. The Egyptian religion was focused on Life, which would determine a person's After Life. The initiations were used to reveal to the initiates their True Identity as Source manifested in a human form. The Great Pyramid provided this sound frequency, this power, and this Truth. We need to realize that this Power of Source is inside of us.[40]

Source creates Souls as sparks that are hurled out from Itself. The Cosmic Creator of all is this immense Energy of Divine Love in constant rotation, from which these sparks are propelled out into the universe. These sparks of Divine Energy are Source individualized sent out to learn, explore, and come to a knowingness of their true identity. While the Soul is out living its individuality, this information is sent back to Source, and this is how it can experience Itself while on the numerous journeys. These divine journeys are an advantage to the Soul.[41] Source hides Itself in the human form. Humanity gets attached to the temporal body, the events, and the narrative of the human journey and forgets its true identity as this expansive Divine splendor.[42] The Sacred Word comes to life in the human body as a symphony of Light and Sound.[43] The Great Pyramid was spiritually and scientifically created to expand the consciousness of the initiates during the sacred initiation ceremonies. The person is tested and finds that they come to realize in their journey their True Identity as being Source Energy manifested to experience being in physical form, which shows Soul's Oneness with God.[44]

McTaggart mentions Fritz-Albert Popp, a theoretical physicist who invented a machine called the **EMI 9558QA** that measures photons, which are light waves, from humans and plants. Popp discovered that the light was coming from the DNA itself. The DNA will resonate with frequencies of Light and Sound. Dr. Popp found in samples of DNA that the Light and Sound frequencies were coming from DNA. When DNA comes to a particular frequency, a resonance occurs, and light codes and other molecular functions would turn on. Light and Sound are stored in our DNA, which controls all aspects of our human body.[45] The Divine symphony of Source Light and Sound energy can manifest into many different forms. Sound manifests into Light, which can split into rays of colors and then into form. What manifests has to do with the vibrational frequency. Each form has its own energetic signature frequency. A yellow rose will have the energetic frequency of the color yellow and the DNA of a rose. A purple tulip will have the energetic frequency of the color purple and the DNA of a tulip. All is Source Light and Sound energy, yet with unique signature frequencies.[46] The human body has an etheric crystalline structure, which is encoded into the DNA. The crystalline structure allows for connection with Source Infinite Love Frequency Vibration.[47] Animals and plants radiate Light at a certain level, and humans also radiate out Light at a certain frequency. DNA uses frequencies to send information to areas of the body, and then it loops back to tell the human body whether anything needs to be genetically adjusted.[48]

Light spirals upward and downward in oscillation frequencies and vibrational tones, which are called electromagnetic waves. The octaves produce the spectrum of light.[49] The number seven relates to "frequency of light" and shows up as seven colors; each color of the seven rays (rainbow colors and colors of human chakra system) has a unique Sound related to each color. Light is Sound and Sound is Light.[50] When a Soul wakes up to the expression of their true identity, they realize that their Light, their frequency, affects humanity by releasing this "spiritual energy" to all. Even though humanity may not be awake enough to feel this higher frequency, it nonetheless radiates outward in a Loving Vibration in order to help awaken other Souls. We are love magnets, and we naturally are attracted to a harmonious and loving energetic vibrational frequency. We are sacred Souls covered in flesh. We need to remember that we are powerful beings of Divine Light and Sound.[51] Delores Cannon, a hypnotherapist, during a hypnosis session explains how a client under hypnosis shares the experience of being Light and then becoming a "dot or spark" of Source. A beam of Light carries her energy into manifestation in the physical realm as a physical form. The Light energetic frequency is slowed down until it manifests and becomes a physical being.[52]

In 2001, the world population of 78 percent calibrated below the level of 200, which is the "Level of Integrity." Most people are not awake and aware of the fact that Divine Source is in everything and everyone.[53] When there is kind and positive thought vibration, there is a higher calibrated frequency. An angry and negative thought will calibrate at a lower level of frequency.[54] Everything comes from the Primordial Sound of Source. Vibrations are then created from this Primordial Sound. These vibrations move into densities, which manifest into lighter and lower frequencies.[55] The human form is a cover that hides Source Light. A wise Soul will discover the hidden treasure within.[56] Why is it important to come closer to the Truth about one's True Identity? Hawkins explains how the higher the vibrational frequency of a person is, the more this will "counterbalance" the individuals on this planet who are at low-vibrational negative levels. If there was no one at a higher level of awareness, this planet would end due to hatred, and many nations have atomic weapons. People waking up to their True Identity is a gift to themselves and to humanity.[57]

Through Delores Cannon's work of being a hypnotherapist, she found that recently she was finding clients who had only been as light beings in energetic form and not had any physical life before. Many Souls have come into physical form that have only been energy, which ranges based on the level of vibration from different particular densities.[58] We are all here because of the Divine Decree of Source to know we are One with God and we are God. We learn of our manifestation powers to create in our lives. Humanity is a race of Gods learning to be Gods. We come from the Light, so we are the Light. We are made of Source Light. We are Light Ambassadors. We come to understand the significance of Light and Sound Frequency Energy, and this shows Soul's Oneness with God.[59]

God Realization is a reality that pervades all life and sees everything as Divine Creator God within and enjoying its unique expression. A person has the ability to step into this higher awareness that they are Source Energy in human form at any time.[60] Dr. Paul Masters speaks of our unity with Source: "I am prosperous already, because I am ONE with the ALL-CREATING UNIVERSE SOURCE of all things – the God within me."[61] Psalms in the Bible is not written by one author and was penned over the course of several centuries. In Psalms, it states how humanity is a race of gods who are royal decedents of Source.[62] People are asleep and slumbering to the reality of their true identity. Humanity is hypnotized by the reality of the senses and therefore unable to see clearly this dazzling splendid Light that is our true likeness. Everything is expressed as this brilliancy of Light. We are surrounded in Source Light Frequency. The universe receives potent Light by receiving Source's Light Pulsations.[63]

Jesus makes a bold direct statement that humans are gods; he was referring to the text in Psalms 82:6, which states this spiritual esoteric truth of our true identity of being individualized images of Source in physical form.[64] Delores Cannon shares how for many clients under hypnosis, it was revealed from their Higher Self that Source is all energy of enormous Light that is filled with vast love. These highly evolved Souls go to the level from which they came during the hypnosis session to reconnect and share spiritual truths. It was said that we all come from Source originally and we are one with Source and that separation is an illusion; we only appear in this dimension as separate.[65] It is important to note that once a person has reached the level of consciousness that Source is their True Identity, the seeking is done and now True Realization is complete.[66] During its sacred journeys, Soul needs to emanate love into all experiences coming into the wisdom that all is Source. While the Soul is in physicality, it appears separated, yet that is part of the illusion. It is impossible to be separated from Itself. There is only Source. Source is the Divine Dreamer, and we partake in these dreams.[67]

Chapter 3

True Identity as Source Energy

A deep-seated knowingness affects all of us on this side of the veil. We feel this sense of "separation and loneliness" that something is missing. This feeling is excruciatingly painful. Many will do anything to fill this void inside. We all have to swim in these deep waters while knowing this feeling of being alone. We can have hundreds of people around us and still have this agonizing feeling of aloneness. We need to learn to manage this deep inner pain of separation. We will only feel the release of this feeling when we have returned to Home, which is where we originated. We are here not only to learn but also to gather information, and this data is reported back to Source, for we are the cells of the Absolute.[68] We don't lose our own identity, for we all each have our own energetic signature frequency (soul signature); when we return back Home, we recognize our true identity as a unique piece of Source. We don't realize how powerful we are since we have crossed over the veil of forgetfulness of our true identity. [69]

There is a discernment that is required and a deeper understanding that the outer world is just a distraction from the attention needed to see that Source is Within and IS one's Self. Once a Soul has union with the Divine, there is this solitude that comes over them. A deeper sense of serenity, solace, and harmony is experienced once this

True Identity is profoundly known. We got lost in the circus of life and now have woken up to the reality of the truth of our true identity. We have to experience the apparent separation in order to come full circle as to experience the attainment of God Realization: Realization of our God Self, fully Divine, and fully one with Source.70

When one comes to the evolutionary level of "unconditional love," then everything they come upon is seen as an aspect of the Divine. We are one with Source because we are aspects of IT. Regardless of our individual paths, let us remember that we are all of one Source.71 The Sufi poet Maulana Rumi, who was a Persian spiritual Sufi Master teacher, writes in his poem "Nothing Happens without You," giving eloquent expression of his relationship with the Divine Source of All. Rumi shares in his poem how through the Divine's Love for Itself, which includes all of us souls, nothing would happen without Source. Worship is for Source alone. We exist because of Source's Divine Love, and therefore, ALL is an expression of Itself sending love to Itself, us Souls.72 While we are with Source, we are so happy experiencing this strong Loving Presence. Once a spark of the Divine is moved away stepping into its individuality as a Soul, it is then "activated" to start its journey.73

Why is it so hard for the world's population to see and understand truth? Only 22 percent are able to know the difference between truth and deception. This makes it hard for people to see perspectives without tribal or herd mentality. It is harder for the population to accept their True Identity as Source Energy, for they have to step away from programming. Many times, friends will leave, family will desert them, and the current lifestyle is even adjusted to allow for this new identity.74

The evolved Soul comes to know that there is no "I" in this life. The personality and ego dissolve as this awareness of one's true identity as Source has stepped into a human form to wear a costume for a while. Source steps into a cosmic play to entertain Itself. It needs to forget in order to enjoy this drama with all the characters that are also Itself. Source has also been called the Eternal Dreamer who loves to experience these different chronicles.[75] Cultures around the world call Source, which is pure love energy, by different names, and some of them are mentioned as *Chi, Ki, Prana, Mana, Spirit, Life Force,* and *Energy*. In the entire universe, it is all Source energy just being referred to by different names and expressions. Everything is filled with this Light and Sound, which are sacred sustenance from Source.[76] Belief systems teach about the science of the soul. This spiritual technology exists within each of us and reveals our Oneness with the Divine.[77]

Light and Sound are so pivotal that the Book of Genesis shares how Source was created through the use of these two aspects of Its Self. In the book of Genesis, the Bible states how the Divine spoke using a vibrational sound, described as Words, as the act of creation. Then Light was created next, so this proves that Light comes from Sound. All manifested potentials for future manifestation and energy originate from Source's Sound Frequency.[78] Our atoms sing the Divine Sound Current throughout our body, for they vibrate to the Cosmic Melody.[79] Atoms in humans are harmonic and atomic energetic power.[80] Self-Realization is Realization of the Self in energetic form as the iconic symbol of the atom is revealed. Source is the atomic energy and lives within every atom of our human form.[81]

Delores Cannon was providing hypnosis for a client, and his Higher Self shared how energy is a constant state of being where it can only change into forms, then move out of form. Eventually, all energy goes Home to be with Source again and will have attained the same frequency. Source is the one enjoying this masquerade.[82] Before any creation, there was Source, which exists within everything seen and unseen. The Divine incarnates into physical form and disguises Itself as a human.[83]

William Buhlman has out-of-body experiences and shares what he learns while on his journeys. Humanity is mesmerized by the illusion of the senses. Any dimension beyond third density is usually not explored. The third dimension is a school. Once a Soul steps out of their physical form, they are able to view the multitudes of dimensions that exist beyond the third dimension. Buhlman's spirit guide reveals to him a hidden secret, "*The universe is a multidimensional continuum of frequencies*" and continues to explain how everything is made of energy. When one moves lower in an energetic frequency, it becomes increasingly condensed as one moves further away from the Divine. This is needed in order to experience form in a third-dimensional reality as an individual. Our individuality is an illusion during our temporary visitation here. Buhlman shares how he experienced directly that his energetic existence is on all dimensional levels and he is one with everything seen and unseen.[84]

Alistair Conwell mentions a woman who had a near-death experience, and she described how she experienced the Light and then the Sound, which deeply impacted her to the point where she never forgot her NDE. The Light and Sound are a projection from Within us, for they come from Source. There is no you; there is only Source. This is our true identity. Light and Sound are just two attributes of Source.[85] Experiencing this awareness that one is Pure Source Energy can cause a deep yearning to return to the state of bliss with the Divine Essence. A person can get lost in the world of seeking, and once found, this wisdom of one's own Divinity can cause untold pain of wanting reconnection, for the person is attached to the **Feeling**. The ideal is the deep inner awareness of one's true identity as Source manifested into physical form in order to experience Itself.[86] A new perspective comes over one, and this transformation is permanent. Once a person has the realization of their True Identity as Source Energy, their personal ego, personality, and personal will forever serve

Source's Divine Plan. The Soul is forever grateful for experiencing creation and being able to be in service.[87]

In a hypnosis session with a client, it was revealed to Delores Cannon that when a human is on earth, there needs to be a separation due to the physical body being unable to withstand the High Frequency of Source Energy.[88] Light and Sound are unified, and the soul must have a human experience in order to have a better understanding of having its own identity away from Source. We can't appreciate the Light until we have experienced darkness.[89]

At some point, every Soul comes to a place where they know that time, space, and matter are an illusion, that everything is not just a physical manifestation. This takes time to be absorbed into the consciousness of the being, not to just know this in the mental but to have a deep knowingness in the heart that accepts it all as love. Creator loves us so much to let us have free will to choose, to have the experience of individuality, to feel what darkness is like, even though we are pure Source Light.[90] The person who has evolved enough to recognize that all is Source Frequency will see themselves as a Divine expression in a body living a physical life. This outward body is just a form, not the true reality of Source Vibrational Energy inhabiting the human. What people are interacting with is the "personality" when talking to this evolved awakened Soul. We interact with all these personalities, not realizing what is deep within that provides the Soul Energy to articulate itself. There is no separation, only the narrowed perception that a person expressing their unique Energetic Signature Frequency is separate from Source. Only Source exists; we are just slices from the same loaf of bread.[91]

CHAPTER 4

Hidden Truths of Our True Identity

We are in a Quantum Field experiencing energy. Everything is energy constantly moving, and we have an energetic Sound Current that fills the body. We are having the human experience by what we are thinking, feeling, and encountering physicality. We hold the Power of Source Energy. Our DNA is the same as God. We are not what we were told by any system. We are Source Energy, and when this becomes a deep understanding and shifts our conceptual reality to the True Reality, then everything starts to change. We come to know that we are there already! Everything is consciousness and is resonating as different forms. We don't have to go anywhere. We are already Everywhere. The Ultimate nonlocal field is consciousness because it is everywhere due to its Omnipresent quality. Each person is energy, which is eternal and infinite, for that is who we are. It is important to know this and accept it. There is nothing you have to get to; it is your birthright.

    The atoms in our body spin in a spiral, from the Microcosm to the Macrocosm, the galaxies, and beyond. Everything in the universe moves in a spiral formation, which creates a vibration, a sound. Atomic energy is our true energetic nature; it is just covered by a human form. Our human bodies emit Light from all these atoms spinning inside us, which is known by several names such as the Light Body, Aura, etheric body, the I AM, also called the Nuri Sarup in Sanskrit. Light and Sound energy is the foundation of this universe, and the ancient Greeks, Egyptians, Hindus, Buddhists, Qabbalah, Persians, and many more belief systems knew of this esoteric wisdom. The ancient texts guide us to this path toward realization of our true identity of Source Energy individualized into human form.

We are a unique expression of Source, and each Soul has its own energetic signature frequency. Source spins off sparks of Itself to bring life to Souls in order for them to start their cosmic journeys. Source is this Primordial Sound, this Celestial Music, the Harmonic Resonance, Mystical Melody, Sound Current, Light and Sound frequencies, Divine Symphony, Ceaseless Music, Divine Ocean of Love, God's Voice, the Word, to name a few. There is only Source experiencing Itself in many disguising forms. Being an aspect of Source is what makes us Immortal, Eternal, and pure Divine Source Essence. This sacred melodious music radiates out into the universe, and this Divine Frequency is heard by the Soul. All creation expresses itself from Source Energy, the vibratory musical rays that form a blissful musical melody that sustains the manifested and unmanifested in the universe.

Primordial Sound waves create the light spectrum, which creates geometric patterns and then creates the formation of different life forms in the universe. All life forms are made up of atoms. What makes the atom so sacred? Atoms are Source in manifested form, and due to the movement of electrons and protons around the nucleus, they cause sound vibrations. The Primordial Sound plays the loving, harmonious music out into the cosmos, and this creates and sustains this universe. The human voice is able to sing at several octaves to create sounds. We can create music with our voice. Therefore, Source is manifesting in human form and able to be a musical instrument with the voice. So here we have vibrational sound from our voice and words creating light frequencies of high and low levels. This is why the ancient belief systems knew how sacred the human temple was, for it was housing Source Light and Sound Energy.

The Eastern monks and many Western monks sing and chant with their voice, even today in many places around the world, just as the Ancient Egyptian priests and priestesses did long ago in the Great Pyramid. The human voice is able to create many different sound frequencies, which cause different vibrational levels, and this affects the consciousness. It has been revealed that the Egyptian hieroglyphs are an acoustic language. The hieroglyphs are created and manifested into physical form from vocal sounds. We live in this cosmic energy of vibratory harmonic music that serenades our Soul and provides creation.

Realization of the Self is Self-Realization. This is awareness of knowing one's true identity as Source atomic energy. God Realization is the deep state of beingness with the knowledge that we are One with God, for we are God. One walks through life with this reality that all is Source manifesting and interacting with life. It is a higher state of being, a new way of viewing the ordinary and seeing the Divine in All. Humanity is sleeping while in this reality of Divine Oneness. This three-dimensional reality is a school, and we are in class. All students are welcome to take the path toward higher wisdoms, yet the playground in school distracts many people. We have been told over the ages by many spiritual masters of our true identity, yet if the masses were directly told, they would say it is a sacrilege to claim our true heritage and identity as Source. Humanity has free will, and each has their own opportunity to take the path toward Home and a deeper understanding of the hidden truths of our True Identity. We are allowed to take the short way home or the long way home. Either way, the Divine likes to enjoy all the amusement rides along the way.

Chapter 5

Know Thyself as Divinity

Everything in the physical world can be manipulated, yet energy cannot be manipulated. Energy is felt; we feel the energetic sense of what is happening energetically. We are on this planet to defy the impossible. We need to be at the level where we see beyond the physical reality and know the true reality is not physical. We don't realize that many times we can be in an energetic battle. The greatest weapon to use is Love. We are not here to fit in; we are here to shine. We are here to be ourselves. We need to break free from anything that imprisons us. Breaking free is now occurring for many of us on the planet at this time. It is arriving back to our energetic resonance, to the knowingness of our own heart and what we know as the truth of our own identity. The physical world is a show and not the true identity. The choice is always available to you. We choose our thoughts, our beliefs, our behaviors. Let us choose. Let us move beyond the barriers. Let us see that many times we only see barriers yet there are ways around them.

What if anything is possible? It's very possible that what appears to be a barrier is in our perception. Let us not be manipulated by the physical reality. The physical reality is only one of many realities. When we are guided to move toward a certain direction, then we will be guided while we live on that journey. If we are guided to move toward anything, then we should trust that when we move into it, we will be guided. We do not have to have a plan. Trust that we will be guided and let the details unfold. We will know and be provided opportunities while walking the pathless path. There is a level of surrender to Source to say yes, and we will always say yes to service to the Divine Plan. Watching our thoughts and beliefs is key to moving beyond them in order to see a new reality in our lives, the more we relax into the reality that the Divine is with us and IS us. We step into a new way of living, viewing, and accepting that helps us in this guidance toward experiencing a new reality for ourselves.

We should get use to saying "What if?" and having unnecessary thoughts—those that don't serve us—placed into the background. Since thoughts can create our reality, we should have thoughts focus on what we do want to create into a reality that is for our highest good and the benefits of others. We can also release our thoughts and then allow our energetic frequency/Higher Self to manifest for us. Let us allow ourselves to be drawn toward what is of interest for the highest and best for ourselves and others; this causes the movement toward situations that cause opportunities to come into our lives. That is when manifestation is presented. We will have a knowingness, which is a feeling that causes the quest toward manifestation. Intension is knowingness and is the power that creates manifestation quicker than thought. Knowingness is a frequency and ability to become that which you know and then step into this state of being. Once one has the knowingness of their true identity, they are no longer a Seeker; they are a Knower. They know and live from this state of being and frequency. It's the knowing and being that create this reality. We have a habit of using our thoughts to create what we want to manifest. The true reality is energy. Feel your breath and know that you are energy manifested into physical form.

When one is living from the highest aligned state, then manifestation is experienced. For example, if a woman creates an energy field around her that she is a mother, then people will believe she is a mother, even if she does not have a child. Her mothering energy and characteristics presented to others will place her in a state of being or this vibrational frequency of motherhood. A person living in this vibration will cause others to feel she must be a mother, for she has become a mother. It is immaterial that she doesn't have a child, for she has become this vibrational frequency. She has manifested motherhood. The hard part of manifestation is that people are not willing to wait until the action of the highest aligned state has been achieved. Real power is living at the highest of service, an aligned state. Jesus, Buddha, Krishna, Mother Theresa, to name a few, did not always get what they wanted, yet they had their needs met and lived at the highest service-aligned state of being.

So, there is manifestation of higher vibrational levels of energy that can be personified within humans. Manifestation is more than manifesting material goods. This is why it is important for us to know our true identity as a Divine Soul from the highest power of Pure Source Energy. When times get difficult, remember to drop into the heartbeat of who we really are as Divinity incarnated into physical form. Let us create a legacy, an impact for the greater good of humanity. The physical reality will never show us the truth; only the Higher Self will reveal our true essence of Divinity. Many find themselves outside of society's norms, and evolved Souls will never find themselves in the status quo box. Evolved Souls will always have this feeling of being a foreigner in a foreign land. If you feel this way, then you are in good company, my friend, for the ascended masters, saints, mystics, yogis, and so forth were rarely popular and most often persecuted, and they lived in a small community of Souls that were evolved enough to recognize the bright light that shined in these Souls that came to do their mission here for humanity. We all have this ability to remember our Divine nature. Every Soul has this Divine Energy within, for this is our birthright as Divine Souls.

The potential to shine one's light, remember one's purpose work and goals for this incarnation, and experience the human journey is available for everyone. No one is more special than anyone else, for we are All special and Divine Souls. The only difference is the Soul's humanity has elevated, accepted their assignments, trusted, evolved themselves into the remembrance of their true identity as Divine Beings, and served the Divine Plan in raising the consciousness of humanity. All the Ascended Master Souls have said that we are all children of Source, who loves us all equally for we are each a piece of the Divine Essence.

The human journey is about awakening to our true identity and evolution while in the human experience. Don't let this life pass you by. Physicality is a gift to experience as consciousness. We need to love ourselves a little bit more. We need to love others a little bit more. We need to get to the level where we see the pain and suffering that humanity is facing right now. We need to remember that the physical reality is not real, yet only real while we are experiencing it. The physical reality does not need to tell us how we view it and how to experience it. Follow your highest expression and what feels right to you, then watch miracles take place. Most of all, be who you are, be authentic, and be real with others.

We tend to seek outward, for we are taught from a young age that everything is outside of us. Everything is really a projection of all aspects of Source vibrating at different levels, different frequencies. Judgment is a real issue in our society, for people don't want to deal with their own hurts, frustrations, and disappointments, and therefore they project onto others or look at others' faults. People would rather focus on others' faults so they don't have to deal with or heal their own issues. What they are really seeing in the faults of others is what they see in themselves that they don't like and thereupon judge others. It's really about acceptance of oneself, faults and all. Acknowledge that while in human form, there will be issues, difficulties, and shortcomings. Acceptance of this in ourselves provides acceptance of this in others.

This frees our attention up for higher vibrational living. Life becomes an opportunity for growth, self-reflection, and purpose work. Yes, we need to live our physical life, yet it takes on a deeper meaning. How do you master the game of life? You don't get lost in it and forget who you are and why you are here. You are a highly luminous Soul that is immortal, eternal, and self-sustaining energy. At some point, we come to a place where we start working on our own state of being and raising our vibrational frequency, and seeing the faults in others is experienced by us as part of the human journey. Earth is a school at all levels, and Souls have graduated from this vibrational level of the third-dimensional level and have move onward; others need to come back and complete further grades and lessons.

We have Souls on Earth who are high enough on the evolutionary scale and have come to this planet to help out. These Souls are the Lightworkers. They help humanity by showing them the way, by being the way. A Soul's vibration, their state of beingness, shows the way, lives the way, and has become the way. The fastest way of ascension is applying the spiritual principles. This takes the attention off others. If one is a Buddhist, be the best Buddhist possible and apply those spiritual principles. If one associates with the Hindu teachings and calls themselves a Hindu, be the best Hindu possible and apply those spiritual principles as best as one can and focus on living those principles. If one calls themselves a Christian, then apply the teachings that Jesus taught and be Christlike. Be the way by living the way. It is one thing to know one's belief system intellectually and quite another to live the spiritual principles.

See yourself as a Soul, Source incarnated, experiencing a human life on Earth. Each Soul is unique and has their own energetic Soul Signature, and each is an aspect, a piece of Source. A Soul does not have the same power of Source Itself, yet is 100 percent made of Source Frequency Essence and therefore has Divinity. Each person is a Soul who has a body, emotions, a mind, thoughts, an ego, a shadow, and a personality, yet all these are coverings over the Soul-like layers. This is why it can be difficult to connect to our Higher Self, for we need to get beyond all these layers. The Soul is the power that has a physical form.

It is recommended to get to a state of being where one can see through the veil, sees through illusion, and stops playing in the divide. The neutrality allows for a level of freedom, for once one takes a position, then one has to defend that position when challenged. This may not be possible with all topics, yet several can be turned into a nonissue. There is no divide; there is just *The Way*. Trusting the Universe, trusting your Higher Self, and this is You. Your Higher Self is your internal guidance system and can be relied upon to guide you through life. The issue is we have Free Will, the ego, and a personality, and the conscious mind aspect of us steps up and takes charge, which sometimes is not always to our highest and best outcomes. Trust your Higher Self, then get out of the way and allow things to come to you. Yes, there is a time for action, and when you have done what you could, then you should surrender the situation to the Higher Self and ask for help. Due to Free Will, our spirit guides, angelic guardians, higher light Hierarch beings, and so on cannot overstep this boundary, so unless we provide permission or ask for help, they will hang around watching the situation, and only we have to handle it all alone.

Many times, people will think they have mental issues—maybe so, yet maybe not—for it is not easy to live in a third-dimensional level of the consciousness world. Most of the population is at this level of consciousness. It's not easy dealing with an ego, a conscious mind, a personality, a shadow, emotions, and a physical body, all amid a physical reality. Most spirit guides would say to the individual living on Earth, "There is nothing wrong with you." Spirit guides are impressed that a Soul was brave enough to incarnate on Earth and attend classes at this dimensional level. Everything is sped up and has more intensity on this planet. The Earth School has been compared to Green Beret training. Training is at all levels. We have Souls here training for their next assignment, next mission, next level of evolvement. We have Souls in all the different grade levels.

In many belief traditions, there is what is called a Life Review process after the Soul crosses over the veil, upon what is called death. It is a review of our physical life. Upon returning to the other side, it's "Let's see how you did." How did your life go? You can then see the areas where you succeeded and areas in need of improvement. This is not punishment; it is remedial. The Soul needs to know their strengths and weaknesses. I like to call it getting our paper graded. During the Earth School there are tests and pop quizzes, and then there are major exams. When a Soul crosses over, there is a review to see how they did, and as on a test or the grading of the paper, it reveals the areas that need improvement and what areas show accomplishment. We have dedicated our life to spiritual ascension. We may not remember our goals that we have set for ourselves prior to being incarnated into physical form, yet all Souls set goals. Many times, once a Soul incarnates, it gets lost in the circus of life. Indeed, the physical world is a circus and is quite captivating. We forget our goals, purpose work, missions, assignments, lesson plans, and so on.

We are introduced to spiritual truths, and some of us are too busy enjoying the physical plane. Not to know is not recommended, but not to wish to know is worse. Too many people don't know spiritual truths, and too many do not wish to know them. It is possible that many people see the spiritual teachers who are not living the truths that they are teaching and therefore are not living examples of these spiritual teachings. We are to focus on the spirit of the paths, not the cultural frameworks. True spirituality is not based upon human-made traditions or made-up rules. True spirituality provides freedom, not control over people.

Quantum physicists state that the entire universe is energy just vibrating at different speeds and when energy slows down, it materializes into form. People are starting to read the energy level of others. How does one do this? How do you feel when you are with someone? Do you feel light and happy, or do you feel anxiety and a heaviness? Do you feel good when you are with this person? Or do you not feel well and uncomfortable with this person? You have just completed an energetic reading on this person. Energy does not lie. Read their energy and you will know whether to spend more time with or avoid these people. Regardless of what they say, go exclusively on how you feel. This is your Higher Self, your internal guidance system you are tapping into to help with navigation in this physical world. Learn to trust this navigation, for it has saved people many a time from insincere and negative people disguised as being outwardly friendly. There is nothing wrong with being cautious when interacting with others.

We don't get to choose what people do to us. We can only choose how we handle them and the situation. Deception is a big issue when being down here in the lower worlds. So many people are not awake and unaware, and they don't realize they cause so much heartache for others. Ignorance and influence are real things that cause others to act in a way that is unconscious. Forgive them anyway.

It does not mean that we don't talk with them about their behavior toward us, whether by letter or over the phone. No one is to be a doormat to another person. It does not mean that when we forgive them; they can stay in our life and continue the abuse, betrayal, or any other hurtful behavior toward us. Many times, it is best to love them, but from a distance. Forgiveness is acceptance of what happened yet not condoning, then moving forward. Sometimes, moving forward requires stepping away and no longer walking on the same path with them in our life. Many times, a person needs to walk a life path away from a person who causes pain, suffering, judgment, drama, and heartache for self-preservation and maintaining healthy boundaries. This can even include family members. Unhealthy relationships are best to be removed regardless of who they are, and the courage to walk away provides the peace enjoyed after they are gone. Forgiveness frees us from the hurtful energy and then moves us forward toward sincere people who genuinely care and want the best for us. Be with people who are awake and aware of how their actions affect others.

Be aware of how you feel when you are with others. Let this be your guide. Your feeling will tell you to you move toward or move away. Life is happening for us and not to us. All life experiences are for growth and an opportunity for empowerment. Some people make it very hard for us to be a spiritual person, and so we are put to the test to accept that we can't change people's behaviors. Yet we do have the power to move onward toward a better situation, where we are treated with kindness and respect. Don't forget: there is an aspect of you that knows no matter what you go through, you get through it. Trauma and heartache are a complication of being in the physical and part of the human journey. We have the courage to do this mission. Be a leader at this time by being the example to others. We are a lighthouse for humanity, and sometimes our light will wake people up from their sleep. We have the power to awaken people. Love is the highest power. Step out each day, enjoy the ride, and let us just do what is in front of us as best we can: learning to be at peace with all that is and, when situations come up, our mastery is tested. We are allowed to be human and vent, yet we should not hurt another's feelings. Expression of feelings can be taken by the other person incorrectly, and we can't control that. Yet it is best to let the other person know that we are sharing what is in our heart and what needs to be addressed in order to clear up any issues. It's ALL Energy; high frequency and low frequency, let us do our best to stay in a higher state of vibrational beingness, for it is all part of being human. We are fully human and fully Divine at the same time, which can make it difficult to straddle both realities.

    We are constantly transforming; it is all about transformation, and it is all energy. Be aware of energetic frequencies. This is an energetic battle, between different levels of vibrations. If we are in relationships that stress us out, then we need to remove those that do. We need to stay in high frequencies as much as possible. What is your body feeling right now? What do you need? Listen to your body. A massage does wonders for the physical body. We are choosing to be treated better, and we are showing those around us by removing people who have been hurtful and then surrendering it all. Being spiritual does not mean we are to have people in our life who take their anger out on us, are mean-spirited, and are hurtful. Let us stay aware. Watch and navigate this world by being the observer. When you shift into a higher frequency, new time lines open up, new places, new people, new events, and new experiences. We are having the human experience, welcome to all the possible energetic frequencies. We stand complete, whole, and filled with Divinity. We are not a speck in the universe; we are the entire universe in a speck.

    We chose to incarnate here. What did you come here to do? Develop Resilience and help raise the consciousness level of humanity.

See everything from a higher perspective. We came down here to hold the Light in this Darkness. Let go of everything that is creating suffering. Trust the Power of who you are. We have got to let go of all that we thought was real. We are Source Made Manifest. Understand that Earth is a place for the Highest Degree Soul Growth by using chaos and challenges as a catalyst, which gives us a broader perspective. We are the ground crew. Feel the energy, the resonance of the interaction of the other person. That is your answer. Follow your resonance and your feelings. We are here to learn how to navigate the pain, so we can turn around and help others. There are hundreds of people waiting for us. They are going to need us. We have a bigger purpose here. We know way more than we give ourselves credit for. We can't let sadness get the best of us. How do we listen? Go out into nature, paint pictures, journal, talk to butterflies, and remember why you are here. Think about your Soul's purpose, the promise that you came to fulfill when you incarnated. There is a promise that you made coming into the body.

There is no mistake that you are here at this time during this difficult time on Earth. If you are reading this book, you are a Lightworker and someone to show the way. There is a massive deprogramming that is taking place within us. We are seeing things differently, seeing things in a different light, no longer being robotic as we live in third-dimensional physical reality. When we are programmed, we are unconscious of this hamster wheel way of being. When we deprogram from the world, we start living from resonance—meaning, What am I feeling right now? Do I want to be in this relationship? Do I want to have that thought right now? Do I want to have that belief right now? Do I want to stay in my current job right now? Stay with resonance and not on a program. This social programming is subtle, and it will cause one to run on autopilot throughout life. Asking for guidance is recommended. We can also talk with our spirit guides, angelic guides, a higher dimensional being, or an Ascended Master Soul. There is no mistake that you are here. There is no mistake that your Higher Self/Soul is providing guidance to you. Pay attention to what you really want to do, say, and be. Step out of programming. Caution your friends and family, for they may get upset when you do. Know what you want, be confident, be assured. You don't want to do things that don't feel like you, and this includes people. Follow your resonance, your energetic frequency knowing. Your resonance will pull you out of your contracts with some friends and some family. Listen to resonance. It's okay to leave them and find others who match you energetically and vibrationally. Be that version of what you want right now and embody this version.

You are a Luminous Embodied Soul. Connect with your inner bright vastness, which is the Source of your experience. Focus on Source Frequency not on humankind's third-dimensional perspective, which is fear based. Your Higher Self is your Soul, which is Source. Join in Source Light. Love is your power. Light is your path. We are all Source Light. There is no you; there is only Source. This is your true identity. You are an embodiment of the Source Power and your Sacred Essence. Your circumstances are temporary, yet you are Eternal. You will always be an Infinite Soul. Remember who you are and your splendor. Your Soul is fully aware of the higher realms. Infinite Source of life provides the truth that only Love is real. More love and gratitude change inside the frequency, which changes outer reality. All beings are Divine Source Energy; send them love. As one raises their frequency, more junk will come up so it can be integrated; thus, one can be able to maintain that higher frequency. When one integrates, then release judgment about this Now Moment.

Experience yourself as Source Energy. We are in a physical reality of Light and Sound. Have a lot of fun in this expression of energy. Just use time to mark events and jump from experience to experience. We are in multiple dimensions at once, at the same time, and we are at all dimensions Right Now. Some will call it the matrix, others will call it a hologram, and many call it the waking dream, which is constantly changing, and we are constantly changing. We are only physical while in this physical reality. We are made of our Higher Self. Our Soul is made up of Source Energy, yet we are made of Sound, which is a manifestation of Source. This holographic reality allows for change in the quantum field. You are a Universal Being of Love and Light playing with other beings of Universal Light. You are allowed to feel sorrow and compassion for those experiencing the third-dimensional reality. Try not to get stuck in these feelings. Then go back and do the inner work. The fifth-dimensional reality (unity consciousness) is being able to alter your reality at will. Integration process is an extremely emotional process. Integration means letting go of judgment. Your emotions can bring your reality to you in the third dimension. For example, if one is sad or depressed, then their world perspective will take on this vibrational frequency. There is nothing wrong with experiencing sadness, for this is part of the human experience.

In the fifth-dimensional reality, we manifest using vibrational resonance, not emotions. In the fifth dimension, we use our Light Body frequency to manifest. We are bringing our emotional understanding of the fifth-dimensional process. Manifest what you want. Create and work for yourself for what you want to experience. It's all just an experience. All information comes from Source Energy. All things exist in the Now. We are changing how we are going to be in this life. When we are a creator, we are not controlling anything externally and internally. We live in the quantum field. We create from the Higher Self. We are connected to the ego, and personality holds the past traumas that don't go away. We have to accept this. Don't negate the human experience. From this point on, we are learning how to navigate it, learning how to be Human and Spirit, learning how to juggle all these aspects of ourselves. We are letting go of trying to control anything. Higher Self is always in control. We are still planning yet at the same time not controlling anything. Move forward and take the steps, then surrender the results. Let Higher Self manifest for you.

Chapter 6

Vibrational States and Frequencies

Purpose is Being. We will start to move from Doing to Being. Just Being ourselves on this planet is our purpose. We need to tap into our resonance. The more we feel all our feelings, the more we will step into ourselves, the more we will feel like ourselves. We need to let go of this need to control everything. We can start with small steps to start being in new ways. Many of us are being asked to slow down so we can reassess our lives. We need to relook at happiness and understand that there will be times when we won't feel happy. The key is to find peace in that state of unhappiness. Try to remember during the unhappy moments that everything is constantly changing. We won't be stuck in this unhappy state, for we realize that there is this movement of energy states. Then we can come to a level of acceptance and let go of these uncomfortable feelings. These feelings will come and go. Remember that we are not our feelings; they are higher and lower vibrational energy moving through us. Happiness is a state of being that comes and goes, and it does not stay. We need to come to the place where we don't have to be always happy. Otherwise, we will be in a state of suffering.

We are not this body. We are not these feelings. We are not this mind and thoughts. We are a Soul, and we experience these other aspects or appendages of ourselves. We need to drop this resistance and just accept these feelings. Feeling is not bad. Feeling is just feeling the movement of energy moving through us based on our external experiences, which we mentally label good and bad. This energy is constantly changing and moving. One thing we can count on is change. We need to get to a level of not chasing happiness.

Why do things constantly change down here on the physical plane? It is because this reality is not real. This physical reality is temporary and only appears to be real. When we close our eyes at night, where does this physical reality go? Any reality that changes is not the true reality. At a higher level of reality, it is stable and constant. The highest vibrational realities have our highest good for us. We have people living on this planet who are in fifth-, sixth-, seventh-, eighth-dimensional levels and some much higher who have incarnated on this planet. These Souls will see the physical reality yet also live and be at this higher level of reality. Mother Theresa is a modern example of an evolved Soul who lived in this physical reality, and yet her consciousness was at a high state of being.

Happiness and unhappiness are a state of being. Even evolved Souls in this physical reality will experience these states of being and will accept them as part of being in a human body. It's okay to feel; we are meant to feel, and this is why we have emotions, which is energy in motion = Emotion. Energy will move up and down, and so the key is about acceptance and better understanding of energy moving through the body. Let us accept that there will be up days and down days. I'm sure Mother Theresa experienced sadness when someone died in her arms and experienced happiness the day she accepted the Nobel Prize for Peace in Stockholm, Sweden.

Vibrational States and Frequencies

Let us start to experience life and allow it. We need to understand that it is the ego trying to control or manage things for us. Let us stop trying to force anything and just listen to what our body is telling us and listen to our Higher Self for guidance. The ego is not going to be able to manage energy. The ego can help with managing our daily duties, yet dealing with energy is very different. Have a deep trust in knowing that you are okay. This too shall pass. It is a good idea to set intentions and then allow those to unfold for you. We are always encouraged to ask for help from our Higher Self and our Spirit Guides. Ask for the Higher Self to get louder in order to hear the internal guidance better.

Many times, we can have a lot of energy flowing through the body, and it is trying to be integrated, which assists the body in upgrading to a higher vibrational level. It can be scary when a person has a lot of energy flowing through the body and feels out of control. Allow the energy to flow knowing it is increasing the vibrations in the body. Sometimes there are feelings of spinning, dizziness, nausea, heat, headaches, and other symptoms that the body will experience as increased light and energy enter then flow through the body. If one feels they need to go to the doctor, that is fine, yet this is energetic upgrading that is taking place in the body and is part of what is happening for humanity on this planet at this time. If one's chakras energetically are spinning faster, then it will not show on any medical test, for this is not physical; this is a faster rate of energy moving through the body. Many people are going to doctors and having tests run, and nothing is coming up on the tests. The doctors may feel the patient is imagining these symptoms, or they may just tell the patient that there are no results or physical findings.

We live in an energetic universe. Physicality is only energy that has slowed down enough to manifest into form. When energy speeds up, it will cause physical symptoms in the body. Again, if you feel the need to check out the symptoms, please go to the doctor to get any symptoms looked at closer. More light and energy are coming to our planet at this time, causing the body to adjust to these higher frequencies. The body has an intelligence and knows what to do and will let us know. For example, if you feel that your body wants a break from certain foods or certain routines, then listen to that and go with what the body is wanting, which may be a new exercise routine, different types of foods, and so forth. Don't force anything and just flow with what you are intuitively feeling led to do. We have a higher level of help for guidance. The energies will continue to increase on this planet, and we are learning to adjust to them.

Mother Earth has moved vibrationally to a fifth-dimensional level, and most of humanity is still living at the third-dimensional level. It's like fleas on a dog: if the dog is vibrating at the energetic speed of the fifth dimension, then this is going to affect the fleas vibrationally. We are going through an evolution of human consciousness on this planet. We are moving out of lower states of consciousness into higher states of consciousness. We first need to see the level that we are in and recognize that many of these consciousnesses are very low, such as fear, lack, greed, etc. We are here to master this third-dimensional level of vibrational states and frequencies.

The activations and upgrades to our DNA are energetic and are happening naturally at this time. Everything is energy, including the DNA; it is all light and sound. It is courageous to be a human right now because we are being asked to feel everything throughout our day in order for trauma and so forth to be released. The issue is trying to avoid, deny, or shift it, so not to feel that which needs to be released from our body. As these densities of energy are released, the light codes within the DNA are activated. Dense energies compact more over time until they are so compacted in the body that they eventually need to be released. As these dense energies are released, it can be overwhelming in the intensity of the feelings, and then we feel something is wrong. The body needs to have a way to release all this dense compacted energy that has been held for years.

As the body releases all this very heavy dense energy that is trapped, the feelings associated with the traumatic events will be felt. The body is purging this energy. When we are receiving our energetic activations and upgrades of the energy in our body are speeding up, this will cause the clearing out of all this heavy and dense energy. This is why we feel so much during times when the energy is stronger on our planet, such as during full moons, solar eclipses, lunar eclipses, equinoxes, solstices, and so forth. There is more powerful energy, more light coming to the planet, and this directly affects the physical body. The Soul is not getting the upgrades and activations, for it is Source. It is the body that is being upgraded by the energy being increased, causing a faster vibrational spin. Galaxies, planets, atoms, and so on have a rotation and spin because energy requires movement, for it would cease to exist if movement stopped and energy can't cease.

Energy can speed up or slow down, yet it stays in motion. So, what is coming up needs to come out. If we find ourselves in a situation, we feel a need to change and then intend for the highest good for everyone involved. We set an intention and ask for the best outcome to manifest. We need to be open to opportunities for change and be receptive when these opportunities present themselves. It may not be initially how we think it should go, yet we need to see what is in the best interest for everyone. Be ready for people or help to come. We do our best to handle the situation as best we can, then surrender the outcome to our Higher Self. This is not spiritually bypassing; we are active in the process of handling the situation, yet we can't control the outcome. Our ego tries to control everything, then gets frustrated when things don't go according to how it feels it should play out. We do the best we can and then surrender the results. It is a "Let Go, Let God" or "Let Go, Let Spirit" type of attitude.

Be open to what the quantum field has to offer you, be open to miracles, and be open to change. The physical reality is not concrete—it is flexible and is constantly changing—so why not be open to other ways of being and seeing perceptions? The physical reality is also an energetic reality and is only one perceived reality. It is okay to express your frustrations yet start intending what you want in life. We never know what is right around the corner or getting ready to come into our life. If we are too busy focusing on only one reality, then we will not be open to see other realities waiting to manifest to us. There are many nonphysical realities that can manifest into the physical realm. We need to stop only believing the physical reality. We seem to be arguing for our limitations. We feel it will always be this way and there is no hope for change or it is not affordable, so if we don't have the money, then it will never come to pass. Be open to be wowed and be open to the spiritual wonder that can come to you. Say to Spirit, "I'm ready." How do we know that something won't come in and help the situation? We need to stop being resistant and be open to blessings. This may not be easy, yet it does take practice.

What makes this process easier is finding stillness. Be with yourself and sit; then you are able to hear better the guidance coming in. Go outside and sit in a quiet place, listen to the birds, breathe, and listen. This is a form of meditation that works for many people, for they are not trying to force anything to happen, such as fighting against the thoughts coming in. Just observe the thoughts; it is okay. Meditation ends up being a big fight with the conscious mind. The mind is designed to think and have thoughts. Let the mind do what it was intended to do and allow it.

The key is to know that you are not your mind; this is just an appendage to the Soul. The mind is here to help you while in the physical. If the mind is overactive, then read spiritual material, which will put the mind to work, for it enjoys collecting information. Spa music or relaxation music also helps the mind calm down, and then it is receptive to more solitude activities. Since we are not our mind, we can talk with our mind, and it allows us to tap in and find out why the mind is so active. What is the mind wanting? A vacation does wonders for the mind. The mind needs to rest from work, not just the physical body. We work our minds so hard, even when we feel we are at rest: we are at the television watching a show, and the mind is being used. In front of a computer, even if just surfing the Internet or watching videos, we are using the mind. The best way to relax the mind is to get out into nature. Don't worry about feeling uncomfortable; just Be. Enjoy the natural sounds of nature and walks in a quiet stillness. Try to find a meadow or a quiet park, any place that allows for the experience of stillness.

In our modern world, stillness may be one of the hardest things to find. In the beginning, it will feel odd; after a while, you will crave this stillness. I unplug from the world on Sundays. My phone is turned off. Whatever comes in will be handled on Monday. Stillness allows for connection. Now I connect more with my Higher Self. In the evenings, my phone is turned off around dinnertime. This is a slower pace of the day for me, and stillness is available to me. Yes, we all have errands that need our attention, and by all means we should attend to life responsibilities. It is best to set up your life for these opportunities for time spent in stillness in order to hear the guidance. Are there any activities that can be released? In its place can be your time to be in stillness. Stillness can be done with open eyes. Don't worry; the breath will ground you. Any time you want to ground yourself, take some deep breaths.

Let us listen to what is behind the mind chatter. The guidance is what is behind the thoughts, the mental chatter, which is your true essence, the Higher Self. It is in the stillness that we connect with our Higher Self. It is a state of Being. We don't have to run around trying to find ourselves; we just need to connect with our True Self, our Soul Self, and then listen. It is not a state of Doing; it is a state of Being. We will be exposed to more truths as we go through life here in the Earth School.

We are here to learn these truths and at the same time to be able to enjoy our life. It is not easy to accept dark truths about what takes place on this planet. I am grateful for the Souls who spend their lives finding out and exposing these dark truths to humanity in order for the corruption to be exposed and therefore for a correction to be made. We are here to learn of the corruption, yet we need to also live our lives. If one feels called to be an activist, then by all means one should go be an activist—yet not everyone will serve humanity in this capacity. There should be no judgment of how another chooses to serve humanity. We were all sent here for certain missions. We need to be a source of encouragement, not judgment, toward others. Over time, more dark truths of corruption, information held in secrecy, and what is being held in darkness will be exposed. It will be difficult to accept and come to realize what was held in secrecy has been exposed and brought out into the open for full disclosure. All the darkness that has been hidden will be coming out and needs to come out, and it will happen in stages so humanity can accept this and can therefore go about changing and fixing the corruption in many systems that are in place on this planet. It will be difficult for many to accept these dark truths, yet we need to see what has been happening in order to bring about a change in upgrading these systems that have been corrupted. We as a society cannot fix what we don't know is out of place. All these dark truths coming up is part of the process of change into a higher-consciousness way of living, being, and interacting with each other.

We are seeing the effects of unchecked capitalism. So as more darkness is exposed, the more people are likely to step up and assist in developing new systems that are in the best interest of humanity, not just to a corporation. I have bachelor's and master's (MBA) degrees in business administration and worked in the corporate world for several years. I went into business to apply spiritual principles and make a difference. I was unable to get anyone to listen and engage spiritual principles in business. No one seemed interested in listening to my suggestions. I got tired of feeling ineffective. I left the business world many years ago. Everyone seemed to be into competition and a competitive environment instead of cooperation. When an organization or group of people cooperates, everyone benefits. This offers people and organizations the chance to work together instead of working against each other. Cooperation removes the us-against-them mentality. Cooperation is the essence of unity consciousness, for it demonstrates we are all in this together, working together for a unified goal.

Therefore, I place a challenge to any United States, European, or Asian corporation to purchase at least five acres of land in an area of a city that is fairly close, at least within a short driving distance, to a low-income or declining area where there may be old empty buildings and land that is purchased, to develop into a park for the community to enjoy. Why not have these business corporations give back to the society that they have earned their profits from? It's the utilization of natural resources and human resources, plus honoring the customers who have supported the major corporations.

Be this corporation to purchase land nearby to give back locally and create a park. Then build a building on this parkland to provide classes for learning new trade skills and offering yoga, Tai Chi, Qigong, or other fun, healthy-related activities in the park outside or in this new community center. Be a leader and a trendsetter for other corporations. It is best to get away from this take-take attitude and way of thinking. People want to buy from companies they admire. Grassroots start-up companies that are giving back a portion of their profits to growing trees or to other charitable organizations that help humanity are the best to emulate. These start-up companies see the value in giving back, and the customers are willing to place their dollars to purchase from them to support a company that cares and gives forward. These are how movements are created for the benefit of humanity and companies.

In your marketing, proudly place on your product or services information about where a percentage of profits go toward a zoo, a particular animal species that is need of help, a start-up grassroots movement organization that is helping environmentally, or humans, or animals, and so forth. People are becoming more conscious of where they spend their money and which corporations they are supporting. Humanity is waking up to the fact that things are changing, and they are looking for change makers—and this includes corporations. Bring the change you want to see in the world.

We are Divine Beings in human form, and now it is the time to use our power for the highest and best for all who live on this planet, including Mother Earth herself. In return, I offer a seminar to the employees, management, and directors of the corporation together—a seminar on spiritual principles in business. Spiritual principles are universal and work within all societies. I will purchase my own plane tickets and fly to the corporation headquarters to provide this seminar to show how spiritual principles in business are profitable and help support life on this planet, at the same time. I look forward to hearing from any corporation that is interested in this challenge and to starting the conversation. I will attend the grand opening of the community center and then can offer the seminar at the headquarters located nearby on the same day. I ask for the park to be fairly close to the headquarters, for this brings the opportunity for employees to enjoy the local community, and this way the park and community center are not forgotten. They both stay in the heart and mind of the corporation that manifested this into the physical reality.

I was fortunate to be able to take a tour inside the building and large grand room in Stockholm, Sweden, where the Nobel Prizes are given to the winners. I felt honored to be able to stand in the large hall where all these amazing Souls stood, gave their speech, and accepted their Nobel Prize in many different categories. It inspired me to want to help and leave a legacy. I wish to inspire others to do the same in making a difference and not leaving it for others to do. We want the planet to be a better place because we walked this Earth. All those in a position to do so, please join me in accepting this Park Challenge. Let us care for this beautiful planet and all life that lives on it.

Chapter 7

Spiritual Mastery

In 2010, I was attending a spiritual talk, and the person mentioned something I had never heard said before in a public setting. Over the years, I have been to so many spiritual retreats, seminars, talks, workshops, meetings, classes, initiations, and so on. The person happened to be the person introducing the spiritual guest speaker to this particular spiritual community. My ears perked up immediately, and the statement that I am about to share rang true deep inside my being. Unfortunately, I don't remember the name of who shared this, yet I will never forget the deep impression it made upon me. I don't remember the exact phrase, word for word, that was spoken, so I am sharing by memory what was spoken. My whole life has been about spirituality; that has been my passion, even when I was working in different industries. My free time was my opportunity to swim in the deep waters of spiritual teachings and esoteric wisdoms of all kinds: gathering them up, learning, gleaning, doing the inner work, applying the spiritual principles, and absorbing the high vibrations into my beingness. The impactful statement that I am recalling from memory is as follows: **You, too, can be a Saint in this lifetime. It is available to you.**

Mother Theresa said yes to the needs of others, said yes to serving the Divine, and every morning said yes to the opportunities that came to her. Mother Theresa was tempted to stay safe in the convent in her teaching order; instead, she stepped out and created a new spiritual order to help others. In the beginning (1950), she did not have the approval or funding of the Vatican, so she started her missionary with the donations from others. It was not until later on that Mother Theresa's Missionaries of Charity was accepted and funding was provided to her by the Vatican. Therefore, she stepped out on faith, courage, and fortitude to serve no matter what. Sainthood is not only for a chosen few. It is how you apply the spiritual teachings, truly understand your power and Divinity, and then put it into action.

This brief mention of how Sainthood is available to everyone really stayed with me. How many of us are walking this planet, on assignment, on our mission, working for the Divine? Mother Theresa is a great example, for she did not go for Sainthood; she saw the need and served humanity. I feel Sainthood is what happens along the way, while one is in service to the Divine Plan. Whether one is recognized officially a Saint or not, I believe the title of Sainthood or Spiritual Master is available for the Souls that are ready to go to the next level. What does Spiritual Mastery look like? First of all, you need to remember who you are and not forget the Light, the Spirit, the Soul in your physical body. Don't allow your past to stop you from remembering your true identity. Do not give up on what you are trying to create and want to manifest. You need to remember that you are in the waking dream, and this is just a physical reality, yet there are many realities beyond the physical plane.

You are a unique expression. Remember your strength and your courage, and don't give up on your goals. A lot of healing takes place when you let go. Let go of what no longer serves you. It is okay. You can call upon your spirit guides, and they will continue to cheer you on. Don't give up. Keep moving forward. You need to remember what you are doing here and therefore won't get stuck into the heaviness of this density while living in the physical reality. What are you trying to do or heal right now? What are you trying to let go of? What are you courageously trying to step into right now? What have you been hoping for and waiting for? What have you been intending and trying to create and manifest? What is it? What is it so deeply that your Soul is pressing you to move toward? What is it that you really want? You need to deeply reflect on what it is—the Divinity Within, your True Source, your True Identity, your true guidance system, your True Essence—which will provide the movement forward.

Even though there is a lot of seriousness, there is also playfulness on this planet. We are meant to remember our Higher Self and our higher awareness. We are on the planet with many beings, and there are beings here on this Earth to remind us of who we are. Some call these celestial or angelic beings in physical form. These are higher-dimensional consciousnesses in physical form reminding us of who we are and that we are Divine Beings. Allow yourself to feel the power of your Divine Essence. Step into this power within you, your True Self. Feel your courage that is within you. Go within deeper and connect with your Soul Self. What is your Soul telling you? What is it that your Soul is saying to you internally? What are you hearing? What are you feeling? How long have you been holding onto what is needed to be emotionally healed? On the Soul level, it is easier to let it go. Remember that this life is temporary and is the waking dream. Our first mistake was taking it to be real. Is this physical reality real? Yes, it is real while we are living in it, and it is also a dream, so both are true. Thereupon our Earthly responsibilities need to be handled, and the opportunities to serve are just as valuable.

Our Soul is always happy to connect with us. It is best to provide time in our life to connect to our Higher Self and listen to the guidance. Bless the Souls who help us remember when we have forgotten our true divine beingness. Let us go for what we really want in this life. We incarnated into the physical to experience—Soul requiring experience, manifested into physical form. Everything is just a concept on the other side of the veil, until one incarnates into physical form and then actually experiences; then they are known and no longer a concept. For example, swimming is a concept on the other side in a nonphysical reality. One can read and know everything there is to know about swimming. Until one gets into the water and actually swims in the physical, then one really knows what swimming is, for it has to be experienced while in a physical form. Being in the physical provides the understanding of concepts explained to one on the other side of life.

The Earth School is a big classroom. In this moment, take a deep breath and connect with your Higher Self. What would you ask your True Self? Ask and then listen to the response of that inner voice within. What is your Soul saying to you? You will feel a resonance with this guidance, a knowingness that what is being heard is true. Realize that you are connecting to a level beyond the physical body. This is an energetic connection. It is a Soul Connection. Allow your Soul to remind you of your high calling as Divinity. Have the courage to step into your True Identity. Know that your Soul, your True Essence, is cheering you on. You can do this, you can have this, and you are courageously strong enough to accomplish your goals. You deserve to be all of you no matter what that is or what it looks like to other people. Allow your uniqueness to shine in the world. You are a gift to this planet. Your light is needed on this Earth at this time. You are a very special Soul, and you came here to shine and hold your light in a dark world. All you have to do is turn on the news and you will see the darkness and density on this planet. Do not forget your light, do not forget your power, do not forget who you are, do not forget your commitment, and know that you are on assignment. Why are you believing that you are less than what you truly are? You are a Divine Being in physical form having a human experience.

You are loved no matter what happens. The physical reality is only one level of your overall cosmology. We have many dimensional levels within us. We need to see it all from a higher perspective. We are not in this world; the world is within us. Each person is a universe unto themselves. Humanity is looking out into the cosmos, yet each human being is a unique universe. We are so vast. The physical reality is only one of many realities within us. When we close our eyes at night, we travel to these other realities. We don't leave our body; we travel within our own universe and explore. Life is about exploration, whether energetically in non-form or physical form. Both are experiences while an aspect of our Soul is in this physical form we call a body. We are fully human and fully Divine Beings.

Does the pain matter? Does this personal story matter? It is just part of the human journey. We can let go knowing that it is not us; it's just experiences. Letting go of the density of the suffering is what allows us to move forward. This is the Ancient Hawaiian/Polynesian *Ho 'oponopono* Prayer that was a practice of forgiveness and love toward others. Let us allow this to wash over us. It is available. Absorb this before the mind steps in and tells us all the reasons why it is unable to happen. Then we believe what the mind tells us and we don't move forward toward our goals. Don't forget your Divinity. Let all this heaviness drop from you. Allow yourself to tap into your true powerful essence and use your imagination to look at all the possibilities awaiting you. Know that you have learned much while here in the Earth School and have dissected fear, abandonment, betrayal, loss, heartache, anxiety, stress, control, lack, joy, peace, love, and bliss. You have dissected all these consciousnesses courageously. You are not who you were yesterday, or last week, or a month ago. You are born anew every day.

Try to recognize the tricks that thoughts and beliefs play on you. Try to recognize the hold that trauma has on you. From an empowered state of being, you choose to release it all. You can release the trauma, you can release any addictions, you can release the relationships that do not serve you, you can release the job that suffocates you, and you can release the limiting beliefs that hold you back. Your stories are the anchors that hold you to the past, and you are in control of those anchors. You get to choose your state of consciousness or the level of consciousness. You choose to remember that you are always choosing. Every day is your creation. You get to choose what you say to people. You get to choose the limiting beliefs you want to hold. You get to choose the emotions you are attached to. You get to choose that you are not any of it; it is merely an experience. You get to choose to provide more empathy or love. The world you are in is "choice."

We are not in human form by accident. We consciously chose to be right where we are, and none of it is an accident. We are here right now standing on the Earth to assist humanity through the evolution of the collective human consciousness. This is why we chose to incarnate. Everything else is part of the game. Every day we get to show up and serve. Do not let a day go by where you do not remember this. Don't let our stories, our traumas, our triggers, blind us from being in service in the way we designed ourselves to be in this human form. The more we can feel everything, the easier it will be to navigate it all. Without feeling, we are zombies. It is the feeling of the energy, the emotion, that allows us to be a creator. Feel throughout every moment of every day, so that you can create. Do not let the shadow side of the human collective field convince you of anything other than the powerful, embodied Divine Being that YOU are, that chooses to incarnate into your physical body in order to walk this life of service. This is why we are here. Humanity is waiting for you. You did not come here to dim your light. People are only one version of you. High-dimensional beings are one version of you. You are designed to see through the illusion. Break out of the illusion of fear. See through the illusion, which will allow you to step out of it and become free.

Many people ask, "What is my purpose work?" What are you drawn to? What do you enjoy when you have free time? What fills you with joy? Start looking in this direction and then start looking for opportunities. Sometimes, volunteering on a day off exposes you to other people in order to see your gifts. If we don't move in that direction, then these talents are not seen by others and stay hidden out of sight. Many people see themselves moving in a direction that they did not anticipate when opportunities present themselves. The key is to step forward and move in the direction your heart is leading you. Are you going to believe in your own power? You are Divine through and throughout. You can't hide your light. We have just forgotten we are the Light of the Great Light. I am here to remind you of your Divine Power Within. Spiritual Mastership is mastery on all levels: physical, emotional, and mental. Does it mean you are perfect? On the physical level, no. On the Soul level, yes. We are fully human and fully Divine.

Our human side has to deal with an ego, personality, the shadow side, and emotions. We have to navigate these aspects of ourselves. Remember, you are in a dream. Keep your frequency high, for your light and vibration go out into the cosmos. When people put their trash onto you, remember you are the trash bin; know it is just needing to be recycled. This negative energy is disposing or clearing through you—that is all. The body clears it out. You are not to hold onto this negative energy of the human collective right now. You get to filter it the way you choose. All that you are seeing in your reality is an illusion. It is real, yet it is an illusion. It's about our Divinity, our Wholeness, and the complete understanding of our True Identity. This reality holds energetic charges. A very high energetic charge will cause us to react and respond to it. When we react to that potent charge, whatever it is, there will be another one until the human collective has pulled itself into its understanding of its Divinity. Let us try not to take this life too seriously. Divinity states that I am free and have choice. I am not that which I am experiencing. I am a piece of Source Light and Source Energy responding to light and energy. I create in every now moment, based on my intention.

Divinity is observing every moment that we are in. Divinity recognizes that we have never been a victim. Divinity is complete freedom. We will encounter along the way that we have not been in complete understanding of our Divinity Within. We cannot do this wrong. We cannot choose wrong, we cannot feel wrong, we cannot be wrong—there is no such thing. We get to courageously choose the way to navigate the external, allowing us to be our Divine Essence. When you see anger, can you allow it to remind you instantaneously that you are Divinity and free and also choosing? It is about learning to listen to your resonance behind anything else—the courage to listen to your resonance.

Dear one, you are much more powerful when you stay focused on you. Remember your True Identity before you incarnated onto this planet. We are here to shift the human collective out of fear and control by allowing their free will. Let us not use our energy to change other beings; let them have their free will. Allow the natural evolution process to unravel for the human collective. We have to allow for free will, for it is one of the universal laws. You are here to influence. Trust that when you stay focused on you, honoring the free will of others, you open up the fields for humanity to step into. Humanity is receiving massive upgrades currently in the dream state at night. Many higher Souls are asking for assistance right now based on the intense purging that is taking place in the human collective. Light Workers are experiencing the density of the human collective. As we stand in the higher states of consciousness, the boat is rocking, due to the fact that the human collective has never cleared the weight that humanity is clearing now. Many Higher Selves are asking for assistance and have been receiving it in the dream state.

Remember the way your body is designed to work. Nothing is designed to stay inside the physical form. A thought, a belief, a behavior, an emotion is designed to come in and exit continuously, over and over and over, in each present moment state. The human is not used to that and thinks there is something wrong because there is so much energetic movement right now, yet there is so much Presence and stillness. Dear one, can you practice allowing everything to move through you? Hands on forehead, take a deep breath, then move hands down the body and exhale, three times. Let everything move through you, everything. Your discernment will turn On. You are awakening into the higher levels of consciousness, even though you feel caged.

As you start to wake up, you begin to discern energetically the direction you want to go: the information you want to listen to, the individuals you want to be with, the music, the food, the thoughts that you allow, the behaviors that you choose. All of it is based on discernment. What feels currently in alignment with your energy, your frequency? When the human is in an aligned state and their energy is pulsing out and higher energetic frequency is being experienced, they will be able to hold this frequency. When this person does not feel this high frequency, they will choose a different experience. This high-frequency Light and Sound will allow one to get the conscious mind out of the way, so one can feel whole again and one's True Identity wakes one up from the waking dream. Souls are beginning to uncover their True Self by lifting piles of debris thrown at them from unknown directions.

It is an illusion down here and a big school for a lot of Souls. If you find yourself in a meeting or a place, or with an individual you have to connect to, and your discernment or resonance does not feel right, and you have to still stand in that situation. How do you navigate that? Pull the energy back to yourself and focus on you. Imagine that the spotlight of your focus has been looking outward and you find yourself in a situation that is not resonating, yet you have to be in it; you take your focus and you take your energy back toward yourself, into your own energetic field, dear one. So you see it is not about change; it is about you and your frequency. You take charge of how you will be. If you are unable to change a situation you are in based on whatever human experience you are having, then you take your attention and you move it back into your energetic field to stay focused right there. You stop projecting, reacting, throwing onto the other human the dissonance that you are feeling. You come back to yourself. There is a lot that you are juggling.

It is important that you are learning to be a Spiritual Master, and this is what you came here to be. Everything is an opportunity to practice the mastery. Even your mind is a teacher's aid and creates this holographic classroom also called a waking dream. Everything you see and everything you experience from the external is an opportunity to practice your Divinity: your choice, truth, resonance, freedom, observation, alignment, and self-responsibility. The louder the external gets, purging the shadow of the human collective, the more opportunity you have. You are ready to experience it, to shift it, and to step out of it. Humanity is ready; that is why it is in your now. The celestial beings have been watching and waiting for thousands of years for humanity to get ready for this now moment in the evolution of human consciousness. This is what we have been waiting for, and we know where humanity is going. Yes, it will be rocky. Will you drop to your knees? Perhaps. Will you want out? Perhaps. Will you stand in your Divine Power? Yes. Did you come here for this? Yes, you did. Do you get to mess up? Yes. Do you get to stand back up? Yes. This is about bringing awareness solely on you.

This is about us breaking free from any past trauma: breaking free from programs, beliefs, systems, and people who have silenced us. Let us remember that there is nothing wrong with what is unraveling.

All will be okay. The humans who are holding and creating fear, control, chaos and divide, manipulation, and silencing are just as beautiful, and they chose the dark side. The shadow is very big in the human collective that we are standing in. However, the Light that we are holding is much Brighter and is much Bigger. So do not get discouraged if you find yourself moving through a path where there is more fear and control and manipulation. You are louder and brighter than the shadow. You always have been. Practice stepping out of what you are in. Practice observing yourself getting stuck in a world events program. Practice stepping out of it, saying it is not about the world events coming up; it's about remembering our Divinity. Practice knowing that if it gets louder, you are getting Brighter. Practice trusting you. You are going to be okay. You are a bearer of light of the Great Light. There isn't a consciousness that can break your light. There isn't a consciousness that can dim your light. Humanity needs you now, more than ever. Every tear, every pain, every discomfort, every joy is preparing you and allowing you to serve humanity as the bearer of light that you are in this present moment. Hold you in compassion and hold humanity in compassion.

There will be a now moment where you will look back at this now moment and be in awe of what you went through. Can you be in awe of you? Right now? Can you try to practice energetically not beating yourself up and maybe stop beating others up? You are more Divine than you understand. Give yourself credit for right now. Just surrender and it will show what you are here to do. Just know that you are ready to step into your Divine Purpose. Every day wake up and know right now you are already doing your Divine Purpose by anchoring your Bright Light onto this planet. Allow yourself to show you how you are going to step into this. Then allow baby steps to navigate into it without trying to figure it out. You have to let it unravel when it is meant to unravel. Don't wait with an expectation of how it is going to show up or what it will be. Just stay present as much as possible with remembering who you are as a Divine Being and where you came from, your True Identity as a piece of Source. Prior to incarnating you were told it would be difficult. The Earth School is to continue the training and tests needed to pass on the journey Home. You are not here on this planet as a punishment. You are here to be an example of what is possible in the world. If you don't feel you belong, that is because you don't belong in this world. You are here to be an example of something better. We are all here for different reasons. Celebrate the fact that you don't belong here. Celebrate the fact that you know why you are not going to fit in. The people who changed the world were people who did not fit in. That means you are in good company, my friend. Very good company, indeed. Celebrate the fact that you don't even need to try to fit in. Yes, your life is going to be more difficult because you don't fit in. You have so much support that you can't even imagine. There are more people on the planet now who don't fit in than do. You are actually in the majority: you actually do fit in with those who don't fit in. You will find out that you have a really great life ahead of you. Think that the Divine Being you are has got your back.

Chapter 8

Mystics and Esoteric Wisdoms

We all enjoy the different flavors of ice cream. The different spiritual teachings are similar to the different flavors of ice cream. Many of us were raised in a particular belief system, most likely because it was our parents' belief system. Our parents were raised in this belief system because their parents were raised in the same belief system. Religions and belief systems allow for a person to be exposed to spiritual truths and the idea that there is something beyond oneself. Belief systems are needed and help many Souls through the example of the different Ascended Master Soul Teachers who came to the Earth. Many belief systems are created from the spiritual teachings of each Ascended Master.

At a certain point many Souls master the spiritual principles of a particular belief system. They start to be drawn toward deeper spiritual wisdoms, a different belief system, or a spiritual teacher who provides mystical teachings. The spiritual foundation is there, and therefore, the Soul moves toward a new spiritual reality, an awakening, a mystical experience, and a deeper understanding of spiritual truths beyond the original belief system they are raised in. The Mystics were known to be the teachers of these deeper hidden spiritual mysteries. The spiritual students who wanted to know would search the world until a high-vibrational Mystic would be found willing to share the esoteric wisdoms. Each belief system holds an aspect of the hidden truths, and there are others in ancient times, such as Egyptian, Gnostic, Essene, Sufi, Kabbalah, Nazarene, Lemurian, Sumerian, Persian, and others that hold the hidden spiritual wisdoms.

The Divine Nature of humans as a Soul is a teaching that is now wanting to be known by the public. Why are we here? If heaven was so perfect, then why did we have to leave? I spent years asking this question to pasters, gurus, priests, and other spiritual teachers, and most of the time they did not know or they said it was karma. It had to be more than just karma. Does karma play a role? Yes and no, depending upon the Soul that incarnates. It seemed karma or original sin was a catch-all term for the unexplainable.

After having personal mystical experiences, I came to my confirmations about all the mystical research over the years. The esoteric teachings of current belief systems and the ancient belief systems mentioned above were confirmed as true. One of these important spiritual truths is that humanity was created in the image of Source. Humanity is a race of gods, learning to recognize they are gods. This is your journey, and Source ends up showing you that you are a god in your own universe. This connection with the invisible world is a very important step in your journey. The Soul's journey is finding out what all this means. Whatever you believe, that is okay too. It is your journey.

We come into the physical for us to experience form and have a fuller understanding of many concepts, lessons, and experiences of who we really are and our True Identity. We had to come into form in order to understand what it means to be a Divine Being. This is my understanding of why Souls incarnate into the physical form, and many ancient and current belief systems all point to this esoteric truth. A person may spend a lifetime or many until this spiritual understanding is revealed and fully understood. Spiritual mastership in not just about learning and understanding; it takes it to the next level and applies the spiritual wisdoms on the mental plane, emotional plane, and physical plane (they correspond to the subtle bodies of humans) within the multidimensional cosmology of the human being.

To keep things light and add humor, I have a note by my computer that says, "Stop whining! You signed up for this." I feel that for many of us, the Earth School and Earth assignment were tougher than we expected. It's a lot of intensity and challenges, and it takes courage to stand in a low-vibrational level of the third-dimensional way of living. If no one has ever told you this, I will share that you have worth, you are precious, you are loved, you are a Divine Being, you are a god, and you are a spiritual master in training. The Earth School is extremely tough, and only the bravest Souls come here to learn. Pat yourself on the back, for you were brave enough to enter the school where spiritual green Beret training takes place. This is why the intensity of this physical plane is in place. Everyone is working on their level of unfoldment. Everyone has their own path and journey. We all sat down with our spirit guides prior to incarnating and went over what our goals were and what we wanted to experience and accomplish. Yes, free will has a play in this, and sometimes it takes more time than others to get tired of the circus of the physical life and start on our goals and purpose work. It's each person's journey, and they don't have to work on anything if they don't want to; however, they may be disappointed when they cross back over and meet with their spirit guides and evaluate their earth life. There is no judgment; it is just an evaluation of ourselves on how we did and what we did with our physical journey we call life.

I am proud of you for your strength and for your perseverance. Move forward with your life. Feel loved, for you are never alone. Observe rather than react. Not reacting to the reality of the physical world allows for your energy to be freed up for you to focus on what you want and would like to accomplish. The observance of thoughts puts you in the observer mode so you then can transcend them. The thoughts move away when your attention moves from them. We may not be able to quiet the mind, yet we can become awake and know that we are just experiencing this physical reality. Our inner happiness should not be based on external situations. Situations don't matter. Only the state of consciousness matters. When the pain comes, we simply accept this reality as it is. We handle the situation as best we can, and while in this situation, we can ask, what would Buddha do, or what would Jesus do? How would a Master Soul handle the situation? Many times, our spirituality is tested and is demonstrated to others by our reaction of acceptance, handling it as gracefully as possible, and then moving on. Will we do this perfectly all the time? Many times, our ego will get in the way, yet on a Soul level the response will be different depending upon who is responding to the situation, mind/ego or Soul/Higher Self.

Source dwells in you as you. You don't have to do anything to get God-Realized or Self-Realized. It is already your true and natural state. Turn your attention inward and upward and come to realize when the ego is running the show and when your Soul self is in control of your life. The ability to turn pain or pleasure into bliss shows the level of consciousness. Become adept at adapting, for everything is constantly changing. When we connect to the true nature of ourselves, bliss arises naturally. Just know that the outer is impermanent and will change. Bliss is the energy that responds to life. The sound current is a vibration of bliss. Mysticism is staying in a higher state of reality.

Ascended Spiritual Masters taught through stories to leave an impression or expand one's viewpoint on a spiritual topic or truth. I will share a story with you I wrote on paper many years ago. Far away in a distant land there was a lonely dog. She had unconditional love for humanity, and yet she was homeless with no one to love her back. She had unique-looking swirls with variations of color on her fur coat, so she was unable to fit in with other dogs and was rejected even by fellow dog groups. This dog decided to call herself Love because she was looking for this wonderful experience called love. She pondered, "Someone has to come along and will see this beautiful love I have inside me." Love continued on her journey and continued thinking, "I have so much love to give; surely, there will be someone who will see this inner beauty." Everywhere she went looking for food and acceptance people only saw the outside of her, which was messy since there was no one to care for her. Love would smell food cooking and thought this was a form of love. She was told to leave and found herself eating leftovers out of the trash areas or food thrown out by the side of the road. Love had never tasted food that was warm and flavorful. "Oh my, I will roam far away from this city and look for love somewhere else."

 Love wandered out into the distance. It was dark and lonely at night, and having no friends caused the pain to go deeper. Love found this world devoid of the very love she was looking for and started to feel hopeless. "Why is unconditional love so hard to find?" Love continued her journey and found a group of people singing and clapping with joy. She was so excited, "Surely, these Souls will see the beauty of unconditional love in their midst." They paid some attention to her yet did not want to have her in their life full time. She was fed some leftover food from their gathering, and once the group activities came to an end, they all went on their separate ways. Love reflected, "Gosh, I was so close to happy people. How come they could not see this unconditional love with them? Why didn't they take me with them?" After the people left, Love stood there puzzled by this interaction. Then she realized that everyone was only looking at her from the outside. She pondered, "How will I be able to get people to start looking at things from the inner?" It seems people were more concerned with their outer life and the outer world.

Love continued on her journey and came across a bird sitting in a fruit tree. The bird did not even notice Love as she walked and sat down under the tree. Love started to eat fruit that had fallen on the ground. This bird started singing to Source in gratitude for the fruit and was happy to have received the food. Love looked up in hopes of making a friend. The bird flew off in search of another adventure. Love contemplated, "Why is everyone so involved with movement, so much that they don't even see what is truly around them?" Love sat there for a long time contemplating the Divine and how this Earth had gotten so removed from the awareness of the Source Essence in all things. At that moment, the Earth spoke to her and said, "I know you are here and deeply grateful." Love kissed the ground and fell asleep under the shade of the fruit tree.

Morning came and Love traveled on in search of water and found a pond. Tasting the sweetness of the water, she said, "Refreshing! How wonderful to drink deeply and enjoy the coolness of this pond." Love decided to jump into the sparkling water to bathe and clean up completely. Afterward realized she smelled much better and felt rejuvenated. Love continued on her journey and started to get hungry. "I need to start looking for some food." All of a sudden, she encountered this amazing aroma. "Oh my goodness, where is this coming from?" Love continued over a long distance and followed this sweet, intoxicating smell.

After quite a while, she saw an old sage sitting under a tree on the grass quietly alone. As she continued to get closer to the mystic sage, the sweet smell became stronger. The floral aroma was so strong, yet there were no flowers in this area. Love observed, "I will gently approach the sage, for his eyes are closed and I don't want to wake him." She did not smell food, only this sweet aroma that was just too irresistible. Love found herself sitting next to the wise sage enjoying this amazing floral perfume. She discovered, "It's coming from the sage!"

She lay down next to him and began to lick his hand. The sage opened his eyes and stated, "I have been waiting for you." For the first time, she felt completely understood, receiving unconditional love. Her heart was so filled it caused her eyes to overflow with tears. The sage placed his hand on the top of her head, saying, "I have been here all along waiting for you to come." Then a bowl of warm rice with a delicious sauce was brought from his robe and was laid in front of her to eat. This wise sage saw the beauty of the unconditional love inside her. He had the wisdom to look inside to the Soul level of her beingness. The sage spoke: "Very few recognize the spiritual energetic aroma of a mystic. People are fooled by the outer appearance of objects, and you were able to smell the aroma of the Divine, which is what led you here to be in my Presence, dear one." Love knew she had found her beloved spiritual teacher, friend, and companion, and she would never be away and always close by. It was the beginning of a new life for her, to be reunited with what she knew was true on the inside with this mystic sage.

People don't realize that the other person standing in front of them is Source covered in a human form. They are so fooled by the other reflection. What we are really interfacing with is a personality, an ego, a shadow side, which are all aspects of the conscious mind. If someone does not want to be your friend, then it is their stuff that got in the way. Try not to take it too personally. Short stories of spiritual wisdoms reach deep into our psyche and allow for spiritual revelations. They allow for us to ponder the spiritual truths that help us live our life here in this physical reality. When we come in contact with people who are angry, distant, jealous, and so on, we need to remember they could be going through a lot of things in their life. Yes, healthy boundaries are needed, and this does not mean that they can stay in our life, for we need to maintain equilibrium. We need to remember that everyone is a Divine Being. This is our mission in developing these skills. People are missing the love. Remember there is no place where Source is not. There is no place where peace is not. There is no place where love is not. These are the lessons. There are lesser degrees of love, and as darkness is seen, this is the covering over of the love, and it eventually becomes so covered over that no love is visible any longer.

Love and hate are on the same pole: they both reside at each end, and then there are varying degrees in the middle. As one steps away from Source Love, the perception becomes clouded and distorted. As one steps closer to Source Love, the perspective becomes clearer. Hate is only the absence of love. Love is there all along waiting to be experienced; it is a matter of clearing out the distorted perceptions. We are living in two worlds; the world of matter is one world, and the eternity is the other world. That is what we do here on the Earth plane. Yes, we have hostile natives here on the Earth. They don't know the love here. Their perception is distorted by their ego, personality, shadow side, society, relations, programming, and limiting beliefs about themselves. In the past, sharing about our Divinity Within was dangerous, and these wise mystics of the past were greatly misunderstood. One was not saying that they were Source; they were just sharing the truth of our true identity as the Soul being a piece of Source. When Source sees you, it sees Itself.

What am I identifying with? The ego or the Soul? It was mentioned in a spiritual conversation that the ego is the jerk. I laughed, as with the rest of the group, about this truth. Ego can push us forward either by desire or by aversion. Buddha mentions how desire is the source of suffering, unless it is desire for enlightenment. Desire to know spiritual truths is the highest and best that desire that can be offered to us. Harmony, power, and wisdom we share infinitely, for it is all within us. We are here to be representatives of Source, of the Light, and then we need to be a living example. Our consciousness needs to be high enough to love people and to care about people. Don't be triggered by their egos and vulnerability. If we care about people, then what does this look like? It is good that this is being considered. The fact that you are reading this book means that you are in an amazing direction. Everyone is applauding you. Don't sweat the small stuff and understand the mission.

What is darkness? In the beginning there was utter darkness, infinite darkness. The Source in you brought light into this dark world. How can you fix or clean it without experiencing it? I may not have all the answers for you, yet I can talk about this with you. We can walk through this together. So what are we to do with all this? What did we learn? Ask the Higher Self to reveal Itself to you now. Suffering comes from loss, which can be a loss of love or not loving oneself. The most difficult people in my life were some of my teachers. What do we do when things come up? Embrace it. Don't run away from it. Bring light to it. There is no time or space between you and Source, and this light warms your Soul. The love that we are when we live in a painful past is not bringing the love to it. Focusing on the fact that we were abused is not bringing the light to it. We end up with victimhood. Only a messed-up person would abuse another person. What is the question? Love is the answer. People apologize when they do their internal work, and then internal changes take place, for they realize how they have hurt another. The ego is the one that gets angry and hurt, not their Soul. Some have said that it is possible that the Higher Self-created the storm in order to have one turn within to bring them to their Higher Self.

Addiction comes in many forms, to different substances or to situations. Addiction is escaping from the present moment. Addiction is from trauma, to separate from the horrors of the battlefield of separation from Source. We need to place ourselves in Soul-expanding, supportive environments. People can even have an addiction to making money. It becomes their whole focus in life. It is great to learn how much we can love the difficult people, for they were abused themselves. Sometimes we have to love them from a distance, for mental and emotional health reasons. However, we can see them as Source sees them. Imagine what it is like in their own journey. Hurt people hurt other people. It is good to acknowledge to each other that we have hurt each other. Imagine what it would be like if this person replaced hate with love. Love is seeing them happy. We can be a light to our friends and for humanity. Listen to our intuition, the voice inside. What purpose did the pain serve? Then release it back into the universe. Wish peace and love toward all who have hurt you. The more we let go, the more the struggles leave.

It is best to say to the Universe, whatever you want to provide, my destiny, I'm okay with it. It is important to find and have people match your frequency. Let us be a living example of being healthy and living a healthy life. Be kind and listen to your Higher Self. If a person is broken, mention what has helped you in this life. Let us practice nonreaction. We have lots of feelings, but it does not mean we have to follow these feelings. Let things happen. Find joy in everything you do. As we journey on the path of life, there are two questions that we can ask ourselves that can help us. Why is this important for me? Why is this coming up for me? Introspection is an opportunity to clear away a hurtful past or the fears of the future. Life is like a chess game; we can only move ourselves forward. Let us keep moving forward.

Chapter 9

God Realization

I did not know what true devotion was until I met a Hindu Monk from India—my spiritual teacher, who was in my life for two years. Mahatma Ji was one of many teachers who have been in my life. High-vibrational teachers have an effect on us. This poem below was written by an Ascended Master Soul and gives one a better perspective of what spiritual devotion really is.

> *Your song is your life to Source. Sing with such intensity of devotion. Have the same intense love that the Chakor bird has for the moon, which sings to the moon every night. Even when its severed head is on the ground, its gaze is on the moon. No matter what happens in this life, always have this intense love and devotion. Great is the love fish have of the water. There is nothing like it. As soon as it is separated from the water, it gives up its life. Where there is Love, there is no reason, rules or common sense. When Love manifests in your heart, it can't be hidden. Love should be unchanging, whatever comes to you in this life. I have tried many medicines, but nothing compares with Love. Just a small dose purifies the whole being. You must have Love in your heart, without Love, you are just acting. There is no room for the mind, in a person who is in love with God. She is totally contented, and sees God everywhere*

she goes. The words of love of God are sweet. Love is fathomless, peerless, and eternal. To express it is impossible. Without Divine Love in your heart, your beauty, wealth, and even your life has no meaning. Everywhere you'll find plenty of people who want riches and happiness, but hardly one who wants love for the Divine. Only someone who is ready will leave their mind, may enter into the City of Love.

~ by Sahajo Bai (Ascended Spiritual Master)
Born in 1725 in India

The ego is an aspect of the conscious mind that likes to run our life. When we have seen that it is best to allow the Higher Self to guide us, then we will move in the direction of leaving the conscious mind to only manage the mental tasks needed to handle daily duties, such as cooking and other household duties, and so on. The Higher Self should be the one in the driver's seat.

We need to start looking from the top down. If we don't do that, we will find we are trapped by the world of appearances, action, illusion, and delusion. From the top looking down view, the creator is in all, the creator is the doer, and the person realizes they create. From the Soul perspective, everywhere it looks, it sees Source. From the top looking down perspective, it sees Source everywhere. All is perfect and part of the Oneness. This level of consciousness experiences total awareness. The Soul spreads out and absorbs that knowledge and wisdom. Total awareness exists in the upper higher realms. When Soul gets back to this level, it has direct perception and has expanded so vastly that it remembers more and total awareness occurs through downloads of information. When one is in the physical world of time and space, it is harder to stay in this total awareness state. In total awareness, if you want to touch the flowers in a vase located on the table, you can with no movement. In a lower state of awareness, you can't, for you have to travel through time and space by walking over to the table to touch the flowers. When one has mastered self-awareness, one can be everywhere and connect with all things.

The other way is from the bottom looking up. A person feels separate. All appears to have a personal will. The individual feels themselves to be the doer. The person can be operating in a mechanical fashion. From the bottom looking up a person is focused only on the physical reality and not spiritual realities, which both exist simultaneously. If one does not live consciously, one will fall into a mechanical unconscious way of living. This is what many people are trying to escape from, this way of feeling separate from Source. Know that you and Source are One. Let us raise our state of consciousness and look at the same problems in our life, looking from the top and higher perspective. Looking at life from the top to bottom and the bottom to the top are both correct. It is just one's angle of vision and perception.

If I am standing on the sidewalk looking at a tall skyscraper, it will appear from that perspective as a very tall building. When I get into an airplane and fly over this same tall skyscraper, I will see that the building is very small. Both perspectives and visuals are true. It is just a matter of whether one is looking from the top down or the bottom up. Soul is a viewpoint that when it looks out onto the world will manifest as the attention. Wherever our attention is determines our viewpoint or a point of view. Both angles of vison are true, yet one is vastly more superior than the other. If one can get into the higher angle of vision, then one will continue to ascend and have a larger overall perspective.

It is not until one has left the physical plane, whether temporary or permanent, that one comes to realize that the physical plane is an illusion that the mind causes all forms. When one has a mystical experience on the other side of the veil, one realizes the astral plane is much different from the physical plane. One realizes that the higher mind actuates all form. Soul can purify the mind. Soul has the ability, due to the fact that all illumination and power come from the Source, which makes up the Soul's true essence. One will come to see that it is Source/Spirit that is the actuating power, the active ingredient behind all mental accomplishments. Our reality is constantly changing because we are constantly changing. One comes to know that where the mind gets all its power from is the Soul/Source. When one gets to the level above the physical plane, then forms disappear and become etherical. When a person realizes that Source is the central essence, then they really start tuning into their Soul/Higher Self, which is Source.

Once a person starts centering, they will feel their journey starts taking off. One's appetite for Spirit and Soul is peaking. In the beginning, it is hit or miss. When one attains Self-Realization, one realizes they are a Soul and the generating power comes from Source. When a person attains God Realization, one sees that it is Source Essence Itself as their true identity. Soul is made 100 percent of Source Energy. Soul may only be a piece of Source, yet it is full pure Source Frequency and is its true identity. This is the key for understanding and is so powerful because you can see the whole view. The mind and thinking are just a piece of things. We need to start looking at our problems as from the whole or top looking down perspective. Thoughts are internal dialog, and action can be just mechanical. We need to start pondering from different points of view. This will help with what you are trying to do in your life. Once you understand what you are trying to do, this is huge because it is realized that you are the creator. You are a god; that is how beautiful understanding is, and all at some point, you will get there. Apply these wisdoms and this will change your point of view. Everything changes depending upon our viewpoint. We need to be careful, for we have a lot of power. Be careful who you share this with. I am not talking about someone else; I am talking about our passions or the mind. Keep your attention and viewpoint with you like sweet floral fragrance that always smells wonderful. Try to stay awake and aware of the remembrance of your true identity.

If someone wants the spiritual life more than anything else, it will come with a price, and the cost can come in different ways. If one is on a spiritual path, then one needs to want truth more than anything else. If one lives an undiscipline life, we have all seen the ramifications. One has to base their life on their ruling decision. There is a perspective out there that shares how the adversary will test us excessively and continuously to see whether we are strong and to see whether we mean what we told ourselves when we decided to walk a spiritual path. Know that once one starts a spiritual path, one is open for tests, pop quizzes, and major exams. All is fair on a spiritual path—especially the saints, mystics, ascended masters, yogis, monks, and those aspiring for enlightenment, cosmic consciousness, Self-Realization, and God Realization, for these are attainments and are not handed out quickly. One will be tested in the Earth School. It is best to be aware that there is a force to stop you cold on a spiritual path of evolvement. It is best to commit to a deeper level of spirituality. We have to earn our right to be at the higher levels. We can be out-created by our own mind, body, and emotions.

We have the freedom to choose anything in our life at any moment. We can choose to be a nice person, a mean person, or a detached person. We have the power to do anything we want, and yet how do we observe our own behavior? How much do we want the deeper spiritual truths? We have to be on fire if we are going for a higher level of spiritual attainment. We have to make it a real living reality. There is no room for playing the game of spirituality; we need to play for keeps, for this is a life-altering constant state of beingness. These spiritual levels are not a place. They are a state of being.

How are we going to get through the insults of people? How can we withstand the passions when they come up in our lives? We may be displaced by the first temptation. We need to be serious in order to stay at our level of consciousness. If we can't hold our state of beingness, then we are a servant to our minds and passions.

Our actions will be imbued with the love for Source. We will be able to rise above the most adverse situations. We will be able to circumvent them through our awareness and through our understanding of the situation. This allows for us to see things that were not seen before. For many people, negative self-talk is an issue. The only reason you exist is because of Source's love for you. That is the reason. You are Source, and Source is you. It's all Source and thus Oneness. You need to accept the fact that you are a god and that no one is more powerful than you and that you have free choice every moment of the day. We need to keep this understanding that we are made in the image of Source and no one else. We need to understand that nothing exists in this universe except Source's Essence. We are part and parcel of Source and are able to be victorious in any situation. If we are fighting anything in our lives, even bad habits, then the understanding is distorted. It ends up being a fight with the mind, the passions, and so on. This is not about being upset with our current situation; it is about staying connected and remembering our true identity, our ideals, and our goals.

This is a spiritual journey, which allows you to rise above all adversity, all aversion, and likes and dislikes. Soul is made in the image of Source. Soul has everything you need. You have that power. We don't always realize and remember our high calling. Our Higher Self wants us to go in and take control of whatever it is that is holding us back. Our Soul Self wants us to learn how to handle the situations that come up and to know that we have the help of the universe behind us. Once we understand this, our fear will dissipate. Life is not happening to you; it is happening for you. The Earth School is a virtual classroom, a matrix, a hologram, a waking dream for us. All this was created just for you; that is how special you are. This is a personalized classroom, and the lessons are unique to each person. We need to realize so we can get all this to start working for you. Allow your imagination and attention to work toward your goals. It is important to arrange your priorities, know why you are here, and know what will set you free. A sincere spiritual path is about constant awareness and a state of being.

There are three hazards in life to be conscious of, and they are assumptions, attachments, and cultural programming. We see and feel the effects of anxiety. Many indigenous cultures realize the importance that calmness and a slower pace of life have on a society. Anxiety is caused by deadlines and fast-paced life, including always needing to know what time it is and keep set appointments. A real vacation is being able to step away from time and be freer.

Why are so many Souls on Earth now going for a mystical experience? Many of these Souls came here to help and are wanting to have these mystical experiences and union with the Divine Essence. It is about remembering and connecting to that which we had prior to incarnating on Earth. Entheogens have always been on this planet, and different civilizations over millennia have utilized them in their sacred religious ceremonies, which facilitated mystical experiences. This is why there is a revival of entheogens in sacred spiritual ceremonies now taking place worldwide. Entheogens are not for everyone. Each person needs to decide for themselves their own spiritual path. It is interesting how many of the population are wanting direct mystical experiences. Entheogens facilitate mystical experiences by offering direct connection with the Divine Essence. Search YouTube for testimonials for the different entheogens, and people will be talking about how their union with the Divine or Oneness was experienced. In the past, people accepted that the mystical was for someone else and would read about another's experience, and their faith was based on what was read, yet now the mystical is open to the public. This is why I believe the entheogens have been rediscovered by the general public and are being explored for self-discovery. There were always those in the past who delved deeper and searched out the mystical in order to have a direct experience, and the esoteric mysteries were written down and kept protected for those few courageous Souls. Today, we are in a higher frequency on this planet and now rediscovering these esoteric truths and wanting to have direct experience of our Divinity Within.

We are multidimensional beings, and so all day long we are moving in and out of dimensions. Some days will be up, and then later in the day, we can feel low emotionally or mentally. We need to be okay with all these ups and downs, for this is energy movement. These upper and lower dimensions are within our cosmology, and this is our multidimensionality. We need to stop forcing ourselves not to feel these dimensions and movement of energy. We need to start to be okay with being up and down, for this is all a part of ourselves.

We need to train ourselves while we are here on Earth to remember how energy works. Our thoughts are visible and can be seen by others, such as Guardians, higher beings of light, psychics, etc. When we enter the other side and cross the veil into other dimensions, everyone can see our thoughts. It is better to train ourselves to remember, until it becomes habit and normal when we discuss someone or picture them in our presence and able to hear us. This will also keep us positive about all people, which we need to do from now on in order to progress forward.

We are in training to be a spiritual master, and everything we go through we will use to help us in guiding others who will go through similar situations. Nothing is wasted! Nothing! All situations are lessons and will be used for future situations with other people to help them in their life situations and to help guide them on their path here on Earth. All emotions, all hurts, all feelings, all situations, all of it will be utilized. Do not fret; you will be able to draw from all of it. Energetically, we are all connected. Have you ever been someplace, like a restaurant, and you felt someone looking at you, and then you turned only to see a person staring at you? We feel consciousness looking at us and also talking about us. When we do discuss another Soul, let us make healthy observations, not judgments, for we all are navigating this energetic world.

Intuitive skills are inside all of us and are always there to guide and help us develop. Live in the Now and stay present. Steps for better intuition are to listen to that inner voice, take time for solitude/meditation, observe everything, listen to your body and inner compass, connect deeply with another, and be authentic. Some other insights are to feel more, think less, release resistance, spend more time in nature, and test your hunches. Take some deep breaths and then tune in to that inner voice. This will take some practice. We are so used to listening to our ego, personality, shadow, and mind that at first it can be very confusing as to what is taking place in our head: tuning into our Higher Self, talking to our Higher Self.

Intuition is reading people and the situation energetically. That feeling you get when you interact with people, that is intuition. Your emotions will manifest as the "gut feeling," and it is best to not ignore it and take these feelings into account as a warning sign. Intuition is all about being aware of your thoughts and your emotions, for you need to be aware of when you are in your mind/thoughts or in your body/feelings. Intuition is our way of navigating through our life experiences. Learn to trust your feelings. What are your feelings telling you in each situation? Practice tuning into these feelings, which can spare us a lot of heartache and provide an excellent navigation tool during our journey in this life.

There are many subtleties that are picked up through the use of intuition, such as feeling something that is impacting the physical body and needing to spend more time in this particular area; intuitively listening to what people are saying, what they are currently going through, or experiences in the past, and gaining insights. Intuition will provide the words and how to handle others' needs and our situations. Intuition will be there to serve you and others in every present moment. All you have to do is tune in and connect to this resource of your Higher Self. You can't understand it with the mind. We have to leave the mind and move into the body to feel the energy. We are light in form, consciousness in form, energy in form, and Source in form.

Take some deep breaths, get into the body, for it is easier to hear your Higher Self. Stay in your body with your breath. Notice distractions from your thoughts. The more you can be with your breath, the more you can tune in, so you need to stay in the body and feel it.

Your Energetic Signature is the energy you hold in any given moment. You see beyond the physical world. Everything is an energetic exchange. Intuition is the compass that assists you in navigating this energetic world. Your resonance is the pulse out, from your body, that reads the energetic field. Your resonance, this pulse out, is accessing the energetic field, all the energies around; when you are **feeling**, that is intuition. That is how you navigate this energetic world. Intuition resides inside the body, for that is where your signature is, where your energy resides. Intuition is not your mind. Intuition is not a thought. It is not critical thinking. It is not a belief. **Intuition is a Feeling**. Intuition is strictly energy moving across this energetic field, pulsating out, bringing in a signal back to you; then you start to say that feels good or that feels not so good.

How does our intuition/resonance communicate with us? How do we feel this? How do we experience this? First of all, intuition is very subtle, and it's in the body. If you are in your mind, your thoughts, or out there, worried about all these things, it's going to be difficult to experience and tap into intuition. It has to be experienced in your body. It's energy, it's in the body, it's subtle, and it's very quiet (like a whisper); it may feel like a gut feeling or instinct. One will say, "I have a feeling or a knowingness that this is what I need to do." Or one can say, "This feels right; this is where I am to be." Your intuition is pulsing out and tapping into everything (a job, a friend, an event, an experience, an interaction), then bringing all this energy back into you, which provides you with the intuition and the experience of it. It will tell you this feels right or this does not feel right. Start looking at it as "Everything is energy," not "I need to find this intuition."

It is energy, and it is inside the body. How often are you in the mind? Then go back into the body. Are you thinking? How do you go into the body? Go into the breath. Intuition can be a vision; it can be a scene that you see. You may pick up a signal of some heaviness or stored trauma; you may feel coldness or heat in a particular area of your body. How do you know you're in your intuition? It will feel relaxed, easy, natural, comfortable. Intuition is the way your Higher Self speaks to you. Your Higher Self is always guiding you to the next higher version of yourself. What is for your highest good? What is going to move you to expansion, joy, peace, abundance, and love? It will continue to pull you into who you have always been, that you forgot you are. Trust what you hear and feel is correct. This is why having a spiritual practice each morning is so important in order for us to get out of our mind and thoughts and tap into our Higher Self and intuition. When you get pulled into your thoughts, take deep breaths; then you are instantly into the body and tapping into your feelings, your compass, your Higher Self.

If you are ever unsure about something, this will bring clarity. Practice silence, deep breaths, and staying in the body; then you will start to feel intuition. You will also recognize when your thoughts and beliefs pull you out of the body, because you are analyzing, critical, and trying to figure things out. Your Higher Self is energetically connected to your body at all times. There is a constant energetic flow of this aspect of you inside your body, so you have access to it at all times. Your resonance and intuition are constantly on and working because they are you. We are just so distracted by thoughts and the outside physical world. Energy cannot lie. Use the radar inside of you to read everything energetically, and the only way is by the way you feel. You will start to receive signals. Intuition is how we are designed to live in every single now. It is your Energetic Signature against another's energetic signature, whether it is a person, place, or experience. This is intuition's job, and that is what it is here to do: to help us so we are able to navigate this energetic world.

CHAPTER 10

The Higher Self

We need to attempt to extract the wisdom from all things. What is spirit trying to show us? We don't have to stay in our uncomfortable state of consciousness. We have a choice, and we can identify with either a lower state of consciousness or a spiritual state of consciousness. We can bring our attention inward. It is time to get involved in the spiritual journey. We are playing with our life, our happiness, our awareness. The Higher Self is not going to pull you out of something you want to be in. Why take a toy away from a child? Especially when they are having a good time with it? If people want to be angry, let them be angry. You don't have to cheer them up. You are already Self-Realized and God Realized. You just don't believe it. Soul is already perfect. So you are living in states of consciousness that are keeping you from realizing this, so it is suggested to wake up and get involved in self-discovery.

There is no such thing as coincidence. You are the one who is reading this book and creating inside. You need to wake up loved ones. When you realize that you can have and live in these higher states of consciousness and that they are available to you, that is when the spiritual path really takes off. You will not only be able to live in them but also be able to stay in them. Truth exists in all things. Sometimes it hurts. Can you take another look at the situation? We need to learn to look beyond the hurt feelings of our emotions and thoughts. Ask the Higher Self if there is anything we are incomplete on. The spiritual path is easy; it is the mind that thinks it is difficult. It is best to move through this physical world without being affected too deeply. Sometimes life is like a walk on the razor's edge. The journey is not always a picnic. Childhood is not always a picnic. Would you want to return to your childhood? Most would say no. This is true in spirituality. Let us be mature and not lose it, in our time of adversity. This is the time to be strong. This is the time to inspire ourselves. We will have to learn what life is trying to teach us. Let us always be aware in all areas. We are Masters in Training.

Consciousness deals with Truth, Awareness, Recognition, and Soul; it has no form, is beyond the conscious mind, and always has freedom. You can contact your Higher Self at any time. Your seeking is over. You have found a path that shows your true identity. You have been introduced to your Higher Self/Soul, Spirit, and Source. You will revel in and be so overwhelmed with how beautiful your Soul is that you will serve Source the rest of your life and forever. You will be in service to the Divine Plan. The spiritual path is a way of life. Source who sent you is calling you back. Travel happily and comfortably on the journey Home. Sing the bliss of the Eternal Source and enjoy the Eternal Kingdom. Source is calling you to remember your True Identity. All glory to Source who has done a wonder, the creator of all the worlds. When one has come to learn of these spiritual truths, it is a treasure.

The Higher Self will teach you and show you things in all situations, so you cannot be deceived again. The whole purpose of a spiritual path is for you to be able to talk directly with your Higher Self/Source with no intermediator. Whom do you think you are talking with when you are taking to your Higher Self? You are talking with the direct manifestation of Source. How amazing is that! This is why

The Higher Self

Source knows everything that is going on with you—everything: all thoughts, feelings, deeds, where your focus is, how well you are doing on a spiritual path. We need to understand that Source is always with us and is us.

We need to give ourselves a break and let things set the way they are; everything has a purpose. Many of our lessons are painful ones. Looking back, we may come to realize that we are not the same people we were as a result of our human experiences. It is best to view the situation from a higher perspective and check in with our Higher Self to find out what is really going on in order to see the value in the situation. We want to be pure from our problems—well, we are already pure. We make it sound like purity isn't available. Trauma, fear, loss, health concerns, and many other life issues cause us to go on a quest to Know Thyself, As Divinity. We are here by Divine Appointment, and when a Soul is ready, they will search for a teacher, a guide, or a mentor to help with the yearning of finding deep meaning in their life and find answers to questions coming up that seem a mystery.

True power is not letting anything in the outside world move us from our position of Divinity. We want to reclaim our own power. Wisdom tells us when we should apply self-control or self-surrender. Love, power, and wisdom need to be utilized. We will find ourselves in situations that will require love. There will be some situations where power will be needed. Wisdom is when we learn which to use in any given situation. This is where freedom is experienced, for then we will see whether we are living in bondage or freedom. In the lower worlds, in order for them to exist, they require their opposite. For example, good and bad, night and day, love and hate, up and down, and so forth. We need to balance out duality, which is the middle path. We don't always realize that there is another option, and that is neutrality.

High-vibrational Sound frequencies are coming to our planet from the Sun at this time, and this is verified by people hearing this in the form of experiencing ringing in the ears, buzzing of bees, and primordial sounds, which are the ocean, roar of a lion, crickets, waterfall, high-pitch tones, and many more being reported by people on this planet. These high sound frequencies are from the Great Central Sun, which then sends the energy to our local sun (Helios) in this galaxy, and with all the coronal mass ejections occurring, it is sending all these high-level photons of light and sound, which are high frequencies, to Earth.

All words carry a vibration used to convey the image of that word. This is why many people around the planet sing devotional songs, chant, say mantras, and so on. The universe is built on sound patterns, which are imbedded in sacred geometry. These sacred patterns known as sacred geometry are what create matter in the third-dimensional field. The different sacred geometric patterns create the different DNA for life on this planet, galaxies, and the universe. One of the reasons we came here is we wanted to experience our High-Frequency Sound and Light in the physical dense body, yet we are always connected to Source.

Many people want proof of the Soul's existence. The attention is the outer reflection of the Soul. If one puts their attention onto anything, their life force, which is the energy from the self-luminous Soul, is what is placing a light onto this particular object, memory, feeling, thought, idea, and so forth. Our attention is the focus onto anything interior and exterior, and this attention has the power to bring a big spotlight onto it. If our attention does not focus on a particular area of our life, such as an activity, an event, or a person, then Soul's energy is being utilized for something else that has our focus. See the attention as a high-power flashlight. Whatever we place our attention on will be lit up, and the power of the Soul's energy is placed upon it for viewing.

The Higher Self

We come onto a spiritual path, and we want the Divine Essence, we want truth, and we are going to give it our best opportunity. All that exists is you as Source, which is your Higher Self. We should identify with the Source within us. Source says, "I am you, and you are me." We end up being shown who we think is our self as the Ego or this Lower Consciousness. We really have not realized this in the beginning. We need to contemplate this deeper wisdom. Intellectually, we have read it, hear it, yet this is just a mental understanding, not a true knowingness, deep inside our beingness. Many people want the higher experiences, yet they still don't realize that they are identifying with their Ego. The very thing they are trying to unfold is their Ego, their lower consciousness. Ego and conscious mind are not going to the highest dimension on the other side of the veil. We need to identify with the Source within us. When we start to identify with our true identity, great changes in our lives start to take place. Remember, Source says, "I am you, and you are me." This gets quite deep because everyone feels they know who they are.

The challenge is getting beyond the body consciousness. Our attention is focused on the third-dimensional physical plane, and we do not know who we really are. So we have to go step by step, and the Higher Self starts to take us through this physical life. Let us talk about impermanence for a moment. What is permanent in this world? We are out there trying to stabilize our consciousness. How long will our body last? How long will anything in this physical reality last? Everything is in a state of impermanence. Nothing is permanent in this physical reality. When we are in the ego, the personality, a lower consciousness, it will be in a constant state of movement. It cannot stabilize and therefore cannot be permanent. Now when we are living in the body, we don't feel realities inside; we feel realities out here in the outside world: our life situations, such as our job, relationships, circumstances in the physical world.

We are just trying to stabilize our life situations to get a position and adhere ourselves onto something that won't turn over on us in the next moment. The difficulty is nothing in this physical reality is permanent.

A person buys a car, and then they need a house, and nothing seems to stay constant in life because of impermanence. Everything swings back and forth from negative to positive and has this constant movement. We try to anchor ourselves, and the God that we once knew suddenly changes because our knowledge has increased, and now we won't believe in this lower understanding of this God. Source is Permanence. The Soul is into truth and the realization of the higher worlds. Truth states that all that really exists is you as a spark of Source Energy.

We can then start looking at ourselves objectively. This is the Awake State. When we are Awake, we have Awareness. When we have Awareness, we are observing. Look at yourself as a god, not a human being and imaging what you want to be. What are you imaging of other people? Enemies? They are a Soul too. When we look at another person, see them as a brother or a sister.

Self is the Soul. That is who you really are. You are Soul. We are not the body, conscious mind, possessions, achievements, degrees, emotions, and so on. The spiritual master teachers talk about this condition, and they help their students realize their true identity as Divine Beings in human form. When one is still identifying with anything other than Soul, they are not going to be able to crack this code. Don't be so concerned with fixing yourself, being critical of yourself or your condition. Focus your powerful attention higher than the body consciousness.

We have two identities that are known as the Lower Self and the Higher Self. We are trying to recognize the fact that we are not the lower one, but the higher one, the Soul. We start to realize that the lower self is the conscious mind, the ego, and the personality. The Higher Self is the Soul, a piece of the Divine Source. The lower self wants more information; it is in the body consciousness, being overpowered by the senses, and identifies with the ego and conscious mind and self-destructive passions. The Higher Self leads us toward spiritual growth and wisdoms of recognition about our true identity and spiritual power; it observes behaviors and commitment to the Divine Plan, wants to serve and say yes to our spiritual goals and purpose work, and has gratitude to Source.

We are given the information that this is all we have known. How can we be different from what we know ourselves to be? This is the whole point of spiritual unfoldment. We want to know the eternal aspect of our own beingness, which is the Soul. We want to know what energy we should ride upon, to live on, and to inspire ourselves. Observe Real from Unreal. We need to be aware that there are two identities in the world of duality, and the Higher Self/Soul will let us know when one is in their other identity, which is the ego, the lower self. We need to be aware that there is a real contest going on here. Once one starts a deep spiritual path, they will start to go between the Lower Self and the Higher Self. The human consciousness is the battle. The Lower Self is at odds with the Higher Self.

If a problem comes up and one gets angry, they can try to stop being angry and can observe themselves at that moment and can say they enjoy being angry. They know that anger is an emotion, yet they may not have the ability to get above the anger, or they may want to be angry; this is the ego acting up. One can call upon Soul's energy, the Higher Self, to get over the anger quicker through movement of attention to a higher state of consciousness. Now the anger is gone. As the Higher Self views the experience now, it uses it as a springboard to understand truth in a better way, to contact love in a better way, to master their discipline, and to observe better. This is the battle right here. The battle is human consciousness, and the two fighting components are the Ego and the Soul. When one begins to realize, this is great. Most people are convinced they know who they are, and I am letting you know: you are not this ego. The truth of truths is that you are Soul, an Eternal Spark of Source.

All the conflicts in the ego are inconsequential to the Soul. While you are living your life in the lower and higher states of consciousness, you can feel this love come into your life. Then you can be guaranteed that you are in the Higher Self. In that moment, you surrendered to the proper authority. To be aware of the ego/mind/personality complex and embracing the Higher Self is huge. You don't have to improve yourself because you are already the Higher Self. In the lower self, many people may say, "Why can't I live a more spiritual life?" The reason is because one feels they are the ego, the lower self, and one has not gone to the Higher Self identity. The whole purpose of a deep spiritual path is the leaving of the ego, the lower self, and recognizing one is the Soul, Source Essence. It means the Soul is Source Frequency in manifested form. This is what a true deep spiritual path is trying to get you to see.

You can laugh, but how much can you laugh when you are in the ego identity? After a while, winning a lollipop from life is not enough to win the day. How do we get more? It comes from the understanding of our True Divine Identity. When we are in our Higher Self, we are naturally drawn to stillness, peace, and joy; it is automatic. As one rises to the level of spirituality, one will see more of the unresolved stuff come up and also one's Higher Self stepping in providing guidance. One will be amazed at how negative one was, thinking negatively, feeling negatively, and so on. This person will start to get all types of insights. Then they will feel instantly and may say, "Source is always with me." Anyone really can contact that love anytime they want. Now one is really transcending their problems with movement of where they place their attention.

If a person wants to know why their spiritual life is not better, they will stay in the ego. They may want to hang onto things that have given them energy to sustain themselves. We want the Higher Self when we decide that we have seen enough and are ready to connect to the Higher Self. One will want to live their life from the Higher Self perspective. Now, one will only look at themselves as the Soul, the Higher Self. The person no longer has this ego as their identity. The Higher Self has a constant connection with Source and will view everything in their life from the Higher Self position, thereupon no longer from the lower ego position. This is when the problems start to straighten out.

When we are in the Higher Self, this impersonal is highly personal. We won't find anything more loving, more intimate, and more representative of companionship. Source and Soul will take your arm and never leave you; they will caress you and console you, and they are your friend. So how is that impersonal? However, the Higher Self relates to everything in the lower body (ego) as impersonal. The Higher Self is not concerned with the anger of the ego. The Higher Self will say, "Ego, you are making this a personal issue. You are angry at this other person for that situation, and I want nothing to do with anger. So instead of getting angry, I will give forbearance, move forward, and focus on what is going well in this reality." The Higher Self relates to everything in the body as impersonal. It's not going to get wrapped up in what the ego says is real in this waking dream. Accept your own Soul as your True Identity. When you live your life, you should make a concerted effort to be living in the Higher Self perspective, which is being the observer. We don't want to be sitting down with this Ego Identity. Try to bring the Higher Self down here to straighten all this stuff out. It is a maze; it is difficult to discern an objective in all of it.

It is like being at the circus, and it just keeps continuing on, all night long, and we get trapped in all the rides and events. Our objective is to realize that we are the Soul/Source. We can't force this; it is a natural occurrence. Our love is growing for Source and is growing day by day. This is the way it will go. The day will come when you will be so utterly in love with it, you will want it so badly, that you will surrender the ego identity. You will say, "That is it; Soul is my true identity. I AM Source individualized into physical form, having a human experience."

Please be patient on a deep spiritual path. Just let the Higher Self bring this about naturally. The Higher Self will keep on giving you flashes and downloads until you can't deny this Higher State of Being, this love, this bliss, any longer. If you rush the gates of heaven, you won't get to the gates. You have to surrender to this state of being. Yes, you can strive for it. Yes, you can live your life the best you can and do your life's duties. Stay in constant communication with your Higher Self and it will happen. When one has mastered the understanding of their true identity, one sees the games of the ego. Remember, the physical world is just a virtual classroom. The Higher Self can see all the ego's tricks and all the heartache. We begin to fully understand who we are and can look from this level and can perceive things as they are in the physical consciousness. We still live our life in the physical, yet we perceive the two realities simultaneously.

The reasons we fail and have a hard time are because we are trying to use our mind on the lower self. The observation is internal. When you are in the Higher Self, you are in total harmony with Source Essence. All you have to do is remember who you are as a piece of the Divine Essence. When we feel that we are this lower identity as the ego and personality, we have forgotten our Higher Self. Poverty consciousness is when one has forgotten that they are made 100 percent of Source Essence. These are the steps one goes through from the Ego Self to the Higher Self. When a person can start viewing themselves as the Higher Self, they no longer see themselves as just a mere human being. You have the power. You are the Higher Self. You can do it. You really can. Upgrade the image of yourself. See yourself as the vast, magnificent Soul that you are.

Master Soul Teachers have taught that most of what people concern themselves with does not even exist, such as our personality, ego, and conscious mind. The mind, ego, and personality have to stay behind, for they can't go to heaven. They don't even exist, and since one's attention is wrapped up in them, now they are overpowering them. They feel they are real. They are not real at all; this is the game of life. This is where illusion comes from, and it is a distorted point of view. It is how we are viewing this illusionary and temporary physical reality. People tend to take this to be real. This is all an illusion. How is this an illusion? When one goes to sleep at night, where does all this physical reality go? If anything disappears, then it is only temporary, not permanent. This is a virtual classroom. The Master Soul Teachers will say how they are not going to play with all their students' issues and problems, which is all an illusion. What we are going to play with is the understanding of your True Identity, for this is your power. Pay no attention to the loud illusion. Yes, we need to handle our daily duties and by all means take care of them, yet we need to connect with the Higher Self, then sit back and just relax.

All the tricks that keep one in the body consciousness and the illusion are what ego will use against them. This keeps their attention on the lower self instead of focusing on the Higher Self. Let us use our time wisely, use our money wisely. The conscious mind wants you to live its reality. Instead, take the Higher Self with you into your daily life reality. This will spiritualize your daily responsibilities and your life. So, your life stays still while the Higher Self is causing this awakening. Let the Higher Self bring you along at this pace. We build these states of consciousness when we attend spiritual seminars, workshops, and retreats, when we are kind to people, and so forth. We start to realize that there is a way we can live our life to make it a lot easier. This is the Higher Self-starting to be the guiding power in our life.

All these distractions will dissolve and dissipate on their own, naturally. We are only shopping and buying new things because we are desperate, lonely, or bored, or we need help, and all we do is think of the meaninglessness of the world. It is all a condition of not connecting with the Soul Self. Once we connect to the Higher Self, which is the Soul aspect of us, we are no longer bored, no longer lonely, because now the Soul can bring the Source Energy right in and provide the connection. Let us just leave all these issues alone and instead go for the Higher Self and allow Source to come in. Then our attention starts rising up. We will feel a higher vibration come in and will experience this. We have, in a sense, left for a vacation, for our attention is in a higher dimension.

This is what fuels our desire to liberate ourselves, and this increases and increases and increases. We are not going to want to be controlled by the senses or controlled by our thoughts and have emotions out of control. This will naturally happen within you. Things, issues, and situations will drop away. See your environment through the lens of the Higher Self. As we start to strengthen this connection, listening and accepting guidance from the Higher Self, we will start to realize there is this limited life we have experienced for who knows how long, and now there is something else. We are not as bothered by our limitations, for we feel the Divine Essence. It is a constant everyday awareness of who you are. You are a god and stay at this level of consciousness. You came here to remember and then support humanity, yet still stay connected. We will never look back on this lifetime as a waste. It will show value.

When a person gets up higher, they start to see things more clearly. One will say, "I was silly doing that down here. Up at a higher-level perspective, I can understand my hurt. I can understand my pain and boredom and can see why I had such a hard time." You see, we need this higher help. This is our effort down here; this is where we are just trying to stay awake, aware, and connected. As you put forth more energy toward keeping the connection, all this other stuff starts to shrivel and lose its power to disrupt your state and equilibrium. Let us put our attention on staying aware of our Divinity. Focusing on the illusion is counterproductive. Focusing attention on the Higher Self as a Divine Being is productive. Your attention is the faculty that leads the way to all your experiences. The Higher Self helps you see why you came here and what your mission on Earth is all about.

You may say that something is going on and you are starting to feel it. You will start to sense it. That is your Higher Self, knocking on your door. Soon, you will sense this illusionary reality and will also sense this Higher Reality of Divinity Within. Why do you want to fight all this stuff? If you will let go and focus on remembering who you are and why you came here to this planet, this will bring a new sense of inspiration. Intense longing and separation are a reaction to being down here away from Source. This is the pain of separation, yet you all have the Higher Self with you. Once we step into a deeper understanding of our Divinity Within, we are turning over a new leaf—converting from the lower self, the ego identity, to the Higher Self, the Soul. You have the determination to go and stay in the awakened state. The Divine forces us to continue to look deeply at ourselves and continue to expand. Surrender to the human experience. Stop fighting it and surrender to being human. We need to lighten up about this human journey. It's okay to laugh more often, for it is great medicine. We are fully human and fully Divine. Incarnating into the physical form is a journey for the strongest of Souls.

You are not a drop in the ocean.
You are the entire ocean in a drop.

~ *Rumi*

~ Poetry ~

Poems have come as an outpouring of Divine energy moving through me and as a form of expression into the world. The poems that follow have been created by me, the author. The poems are original and have been written over a course of many years and now have a place to be released out into the public to enjoy them.

Love Potion

I sipped your love potion,
Was never the same.
Now I see you everywhere,
Love sick for you.
I am drunk on the wine,
From the Divine.
Don't wake me up,
Please be so kind.
Dreamed of bliss,
And happiness.
Love elixir cleanse the soul,
Two united became whole.

~ Nancy Clark

Soul and Beloved

I've come back for you, my dear one
don't be fooled, by the world of appearances.
Love has come to take you home.
If you see anything other than love, that is not real.
My wish for you, is to see through
and beyond all this matter, space, time.
Your body is on loan, one day,
you'll be free of the mind and emotions.
All that is you is Soul, a drop of the Divine.
I know who you are.
Your Source is calling you back home.
Do you know how fortunate you are,
to be able to talk to this Powerful Essence?
Come to know of my secret.
Throw off these coverings, reveal the Pure Soul.
Where illusion exists, thought must exist.
Spell of illusion, temporary separation,
of Soul from Divine.
Where there is only the Divine, no thought can exist.
Illusion and Thought
Soul and Beloved
Thoughts break our connection
Mind keeps you in illusion
Soul, stay close, don't forget about me today.

Watch the thoughts, stay on the path of love and devotion.
This is just a play down here, let go of all anxieties,
Come and live in my world
Of peace and bliss.

~ *Nancy Clark*

Soul versus Mind

Mind creates Drama
Soul bathes in Peace
Mind causes Separation
Soul swims in Harmony
Mind sends deception, distortions
Soul already Pure
Mind full of Personality
Soul radiates Love
Mind manifests Logic, Reason, Illusion
Soul has Direct Perception
Mind wants Control
Soul enjoys being Happy
Mind's Ego is Angry
Soul is a Blissful entity
Mind, Temporary expression
Soul, Eternal Spark
Mind creates illusion
Soul has Secured Freedom
Mind manifests External stimuli
Soul possesses External attributes
Mind experiences tension, separation, conflict
Soul understands Knowing, Being, Seeing
Mind, drowning in Negativity
Soul, drop from Divine Ocean
Mind, controlled by Universal Mind Power
Soul, Essence of Supreme Source

~ Nancy Clark

Becoming You

Stepped into the World

Forgot my True Self

Identity Theft

Being with the Mind

Endless Games

True Identity Appears

Love Floods the Soul

Purifies All Bodies

Truth will become You

Constant Communion

Identity with Source

Switched Identity

Became You

Realization of Oneness

~ Nancy Clark

Purification

What did I do to deserve the love of the purification?

Knowing the Divine is in me provides the strength to endure.

Love from the Divine is the purification.

Divine Love is so powerful, it burns away all the impurities.

Intensity of this love creates the heat that burns.

Heat of desire fuels the fire of love more,
as the intensity picks up toward the Divine.

Pleasure of pain is understood when the karmas are paid in full.

The agony of separation turns to full joy,
when the purification is complete.

How blessed indeed is the one going through,
The purification journeys.

~ Nancy Clark

Next to You

Why do you feel alone?

When have I told you,
you are alone?

This feeling is fleeting,
comes and goes.

Can't you see me,
next to you,
looking into your eyes?

Beautiful one,
special one,
how can I ever,
forget you?

You are made from,
the essence of myself.

I loved you before,
heavens were created.

How can I forget myself?

~ Nancy Clark

Singing to You

How can one live this earthly life?
When the Divine is nearby.

How can one continue in this dream?
When the Divine is blowing you kisses to wake you up.

This is no earthly love,
Beyond frontiers my dear.

The stars are even jealous of how
the Divine pays so much attention to you.

Hear the Divine singing to you?
Divine's love call is so enchanting.

The music gets louder and louder
until the Love wins you over.

Don't fight too hard, let the Divine have you.
This is the deepest love.

Be happy the Divine is chasing you.

~ Nancy Clark

Transcended

Walking with the Divine
Effects One Deeply
Outside Noises, Disturbances
Social Daily Life
Pain of Separation
Nearly too much to bear

Going deeper inward
Remaining in Samadhi
Staying connected
Focused with the Beloved
Saturated with Love
United with Source

Acceptance of Life
Human Consciousness Transcended
Deeper Understanding
Earthly Existence
Commissioned Mission
You signed up

Samadhi focused State
Perfect for Source Plan
Stepped down the Power
While stationed here
Present Spiritual Ecstasy
Service to the Divine Plan

~ Nancy Clark

Your Gift

You are Special
One of a Kind
Uniquely Created
Eternally Divine

Before Incarnation
Talent Imprinted
Guidance Selected
Sent from Above

Encouragement Continued
Inspiration Required
Contemplate Fulfillment
Confirmation is Laughter

Inner Beingness
Creativity Abounds
You will Know
Energy will Flow

~ Nancy Clark

Oneness

Oneness, Inner Space
Oneness, Outer Space
Interconnected, Selected
Totally Unified

Soul's Indivisible Oneness
Look for the One
That teaches Oneness
We are many, yet One

One in Origin, Came from Divine
One is Design, One of a Kind
Let's cry together, Laugh together
Ultimate Goal, One with Divine

This world teaches us
Living on same planet together
Each unique path, same path
Steps toward Home

Soul started as One, in Higher plane
On Planet Earth, became many identities
Soul sheds lower appendages
Rises upward to its Divine Oneness

~ Nancy Clark

Divine Union

Stop screaming Mind!

Soul craves Divine Union

Stop creating Drama

Soul wishes for Serenity

Stop talking

Soul requests Quietness

Quit Yelling!

Soul requires Divine Connection

Stop looking around

Walk your own path

Inner Path, Inner Union

Divine Union

~ Nancy Clark

Pierce the Veil

See beyond the Veil
of duality
of relationships
of belief systems

What is beyond
this Veil
this matrix
this hologram

Love Pierces
Love exposes
Love teaches
Love reveals

First see the Veils
Lift each Veil
Rise above
Unveiling your True Self

~ Nancy Clark

Duality

Pain and Pleasure
Duality is the teacher
Look for the lessons
Both sides reside inside

Starts out as a rainy day
Turns into a sunny day
Look for the rainbow
Shows light through water droplets

Dirt and Darkness
Seeds and Sunlight
Creates the canvas
Duality creates life

Extreme ends of the same pole
These emotions inside you
Experienced in dual nature
Shows both are you

You are both darkness and light
Human experience provides this truth
Now, rise Above Duality
Your higher identity is Divine

~ Nancy Clark

Sacrifice

Sacrifice my body, mind, emotions
in order to be with you

Provide me with your inner Presence
You are what sustains me

Life is a wasteland without you
everywhere I look are the passions

How can I go on without you?
Now that we have met.

Restore me with the Divine Presence

Flow of tears
Fires of longing
Connecting daily
Distraught with anguish

I now understand Divinity

Personal life is over
All about the Divine Plan
All-consuming love
Surrendered my life for you

~ Nancy Clark

Ocean of Tears

Let the tears cleanse my Soul

Wash away the impurities, the pain

Deep aches, grieving of being away from you

Never felt pain go so deep

When will my Soul be in union with the Divine?

Painful yearning, process of cleansing

Wash me pure of all karmas

Crying an ocean of tears for you

Nothing satisfies this Soul

Beloved holds the key to my heart

Come quickly and be with me

You've turned up the volume of the sphere-music

Loud speakers in my ear

Your love call tells me you are nearby

Bring us toward union

When you become One with the Divine, there is no you.

All that you do disappears, Divine becomes the Doer.

~ Nancy Clark

Courting with Delight

Beloved, you speak to me day and night,
You are courting me with delight.

You see the tears flow down my face,
I hear the words, filled with grace.

You know me deeply,
Sing to me sweetly.

Your love is sincerely true,
Sweet perfume is all around you.

When the Divine Melody is heard,
Experiencing the Word.

~ Nancy Clark

Destiny

The road that you must travel
was in the stars before you came

Every step pre-ordained
you feel drawn to a higher life

You are known, beautiful Soul
reaching out for your hand

Come to higher regions
it's your Destiny

You are meant to be with me
Release, trust me

Beyond the veil
you will see me
waiting for you

Transformation awaits you
It's your Destiny
to be united with me

Stars foretell of Destiny
At one point, you will become me

~ Nancy Clark

Holding Hands

I saw you today, Beloved
holding tightly my hand.

Experiencing your love,
tears flowing down,
overwhelming me.

Sending a message,
"You are my very own,
truly know that you are loved."

Dazzling lights catch my eyes,
forgetting my Beloved.

Remember, Remember,
Grabbing the Beloved hand once again,
now in tune with the melody.

~ Nancy Clark

Run Quickly

Language of love
is intimate connection
with Divine to Soul

Birds love to be with the sky
trees deep connection with the earth

Keep an open ear,
to the Divine's enchanting melody

Body does not know how to handle,
the Soul crying out
to be with the Divine Essence

It is time to break free
Run Quickly
before the mind wakes up
follow the music
the audible life stream
your deepest friend

Ocean of Love and Mercy
is waiting for the drop

Continue on the river
that takes you to the ocean

~ Nancy Clark

Late-Night Date

Date with Divinity
Oh, how sweet!

Smelled the Divine
Love perfume all around

Mind was dizzy
Ego was spinning

Soul was dancing
With delight

Could not sleep
Seeing the Divine's gaze

Spent the evening
Talking with The Presence

Enjoy these
Loving eyes
Upon me

~ Nancy Clark

Living Image

Divine is a Living Image
Let's stay together
Constant connection
In daily life

Splendor moments of
Love Waves washing over me
Brings tears, seeing you near

Your loving eyes
Gazing into mine
Washing impurities away
Purification with Love

Hold onto what is True
Hold onto what is Real
Release illusion, confusion

Temporary images hold one down
Gravity to the Soul
Come up to higher ground
The Living Image

~ Nancy Clark

Sing to the Divine

A sparrow was singing in a tree when a Mystic Saint came walking by.
The bird sang out and asked the Mystic, "Please stay for a while."

The Mystic so full of love and grace responded, "Sing to the Divine."

The bird sang the sweetest song. Mystic Saint's eyes were wide. The sparrow felt a love wave go through her. She had never experienced
this before and fell out of the tree.

The Mystic Saint caught her gently. Her love for the Mystic Saint began to grow. The Mystic Saint was a Divine Being, not like all the others. With a smile,
the Mystic sat down under the tree with the sparrow on his palm. She was so happy, her heart felt as if it would burst from all the love.

The sparrow realized that the Mystic was indeed Divine in the flesh! Amazing gift to be in the Divine's hand. Love songs came constantly and even her voice changed. She vowed to spend her life always thinking of Source.

All her songs would be sung to the Living Presence. Every action would be for
her Beloved. Her life was no longer her own, it now belonged to the Divine.

The Living Presence continued to gaze at her and enjoy her songs to the Divine. Then the Mystic leaned down and whispered sweetly in her ear, a promise in her future life.

She sang so loud and hopped onto the Saint's shoulder. The sparrow would spend the rest of her days with the Mystic Saint. This Master Soul would always have her nearby singing to provide companionship.

Her life would never be the same for she was forever changed.

~ Nancy Clark

Marked

Marked Soul,
you are blessed.

Came for you,
please stay near,
you are forever dear.

Life is a shadow,
pay no mind.

Focus on connection,
one day resurrection.

Whispers in your ear,
my great love for you.

Kisses on your forehead,
wake you up at night.

Who is courting you?

Your forgotten Source.

Missing you, time to come Home,
leave the playground, physical friends,
dance with me all the way Home.

~ Nancy Clark

Union with Sound

That Divine Melody,
constantly rings in my ear.

The ringing radiance,
I will forever hear.

The voice of the Divine,
singing sweetly is sublime.

How can I not surrender to this enchantment?
The Divine is chasing my Soul.

My personal will is slipping away,
attraction so strong every day.

When the Divine is nearby,
my Soul feels ecstasy.

This physical reality,
is nothing but a fantasy.

When the Beloved is nearby,
my Soul takes flight.

Hearing the sweet whispers,
hearing is such a delight.

When the Divine is nearby,
I am forever,
in this Charm

~ *Nancy Clark*

Wild Ride

Life is full of potholes,
Unhappy drivers.

Life scenes are distressing,
Everyone in a rush.

A fellow traveler,
Comes to say, "I'll help you."

Feeling lost and tired,
A welcomed friend.

New path is shown,
A narrow road.

My ego car won't fit,
Start walking instead.

My friend encourages me,
To keep going forward.

The road goes straight up!

Love is provided,
Sound Current gets stronger.

My dear friend,
Provides jet fuel.

My ego falls off,
Music is heard.

I see stars!
Planets, Solar Systems, Galaxies.

We're traveling at the speed of Sound!
My guides states, "Hold On!"

Ride gets bumpy,
Everything gets brighter.

My guide turns out to be,
Source!

How blessed to remember,
My True Identity.

Journey toward Home,
Is a Wild Ride.

~ Nancy Clark

Unforgettable

Created from Love

Piece of Source

Birthright to come back Home

My Very Own

Always been together

A particle of me

Never forget

The Love for you

Will always be

You are Unforgettable

~ Nancy Clark

Higher Realm

Surrender to the One

You're smiling at me

Divine Melody

Enrapturing Sound

Constant sweetness

Soul being intoxicated

A Love so powerful

Calling to come higher

A yearning created

Familiar connection

Intense love call

Must come higher

Soul desires constant connection

Living in same region

Where the Divine resides

Magnetic attraction toward union

~ Nancy Clark

Magnetic Attraction

Love for the Divine
Causing upward pull
Intensity created
With this marked Soul

Everywhere I look
You are there
Looking at me
My heart yearns

Intensity created
Love for the Divine
Magnetic Attraction
Unable to resist

Love is strong
Powerful within
Surrendered to the Sound
Enraptured with Love

~ Nancy Clark

Being in Love

To be in Love
Feeling Loved
Everything Changes
Perspective of Love

One dances along
A skip in the step
Playfulness
Words of Love

Deep Warmth
Completeness
Feeling Special
It shows in the face

Laughter and smiles
Deep gazes of Love
Getting lost in Loving Eyes
Oh, Beloved, I'm yours

~ Nancy Clark

Love Letter

How exciting
Received a
Love Letter

Butterflies in tummy
Bliss in words
Feeling Special

Love grows
Yearning continues
Hearing your voice

Lofted away
Love connection
Feeling Perfection

~ Nancy Clark

Wearing Glasses

You're wearing glasses

Your view is
World of Appearances

Misery, illusion
loneness, separation
Lenses of Tears

Teacher of Love
Removes glasses

Third Eye opened
Clear View

Flood of Love
Surrender came
Bliss arrived
Residency with Divine

~ Nancy Clark

Love toward You

Why are you looking at the world?
You could be gazing at the eyes of
Love toward you

Don't be fooled by
World of Appearances

Come, hold my hand

Let me take you, Home

You are Royalty
Your Divine Source
Awaits your arrival

Why are you
Wasting your time
With illusions?

Have Eternal Bliss
Continual Companionship

Don't tally dear one
Come Home

~ Nancy Clark

Secret Love Affair

Internal Conversations
No one suspects
Oneness with the Divine

That Look of Love
Internal Gaze
Quietness Comes

Unspoken whispers
Flower fragrances
Love calmness

Complete Surrender
Can't live without
Secret Love Affair

~ Nancy Clark

Quietness

Contemplation
Reveals
Deeper Meaning

Inner Peace
Reveals
Deeper Insights

Calmness
Settles in
Deeper Revelations

Quietness
Offers
Contemplative Life

Solitude
Necessary
Being with Beloved

Inward Gaze
Quiet Conversations
The Divine Manifests

~ Nancy Clark

Do You Hear?

I hear "Your Voice" Inside

Silent Connection

Peaceful, Tranquil, Loving

Verbal Silence

Always Available

Accessible Within

Secret Mystery

Wonder of Wonders

Soul is Graced

Higher Journey

Wisdom Abounds

Questions are Answered

Love Path toward Home

~ Nancy Clark

Conversation

Where did you go?

I was there all along.

Why can't eyes see you?

Open Spiritual Eye.

When will we be together?

Beloved is always with you.

How was Soul selected?

Source Chose You.

What is the goal?

Soul come Home.

Why do I feel alone?

Hold my hand.

Where does Fear originate?

Keeping company with the Mind.

Why so many lessons?

School of Unfoldment.

How can Soul Merge with Truth?

Continual Connection with Beloved.

What is True Love?

Attention, Saturated, Consumed, Surrendered.

Where is Home?
100% Communion with Divine.

When can Soul go Home?

In this Present Moment,
Current Conversation
You are Home.

~ Nancy Clark

Fresh Flowers

The Aroma is overwhelming

Makes my head swirl

Mind is now empty, no thoughts

Flora Water is all around

Permeating, intoxicating, purifying

Divine has provided these special flowers

These colors never seen on Earth

"This is the smell of Divine Love"

Taken away far from the Earth

Divine Ambrosia removes the weights

Floating ever upward towards Love

Buzzing, Whirling Vibrations, Serene Calmness

Divine Aroma causes one to let go

Allow the Third Eye to open

View beyond the veil

You'll never be the same

Fresh Flowers from The Divine

Now enjoy them every moment.

~ Nancy Clark

Medicine

Love is the medicine,
cures all completely.

Cleanses the wounds,
of pain, of time,
of attachment, of passions.

Purify the wounds,
Permanent healing occurs,
no need to come back.

Take the medicine of connection,
side effects include,
loss of illusion,
loss of delusion,
plenty of infusion,
of the Love inclusion.

~ *Nancy Clark*

Divine Elixir

I got drunk today, what could I do?
Source kept pouring Love into my glass.
The whole world disappears.
All I feel is the warming effects of the Spirit Elixir.
That warm, fuzzy, relaxing sensation of the brew.
The whole world looks different.
Who cares!
Let's have another glass of the Love ambrosia.
My drinking buddy is my dearest friend and companion.
The Inner Presence keeps me under the influence.
In my drunken stupor, people see me smiling and feel I am a fool.
My soul can't get enough of this ecstasy.
Please more!
I have to continue to get more.
Don't stop pouring!
I can have as much as I want?
On my goodness...
The Love is always flowing, just keep drinking, keep drinking.
I don't want the effects to wear off.
The soul keeps drinking, the world begins to fade away.
Don't want to be sober anymore, world please disappear.
Only desire to feel the effects of this wine for the Soul.
Shakes come when the effects wear off.
Need to get back to the Mystical lounge.
A moment without The Divine is agony.

World is a crazy place.
Requires the Love to not let it affect me.
Let the world spin,
Eyes glazed over by the Divine, releases the effects.
Oh, Blessed One,
Please don't stop pouring.
The abundance is overwhelming,
Let the Bliss rain down,
Want to be drenched, soak me with your love.

~ Nancy Clark

Heartache

Squeezing of the heart
Painful Tears
Tight stomach knots
Gripping Emotions

Heart knows
Intuition is discovered
Pain becomes wisdom
Forgiveness realized

A wise teacher
Opens the heart
Loves fully
Laughs completely

Pain teaches us
Learn to listen
To the heart
Who guides

Heart is
A wise teacher
Who loves life
Raises you higher

~ Nancy Clark

Gaia

Mother Earth
Loving Planet
Sustaining Life
Nurturing Us

Destroying the Forests
Animals Disappearing
Polluted Oceans
Crying for Help

Herbs, Plants, Soil
Birds, Animals, Humans
Gaia Loves Us All
Appreciate her beauty

Gaia Earth
Taken for granted
Love Her Back
Blow her a kiss today

Step into the role
Ecology action
Action for the planet
Love Mother Gaia back

~ Nancy Clark

Awakening

I heard the Falcon crying today
This One had lost its way
Alone, feeling forgotten
Grieving, wailing so loud
Crying for help

Then a Spiritual Power
Came into the Falcon's Life
This Oneness began to sing
Soaring through the air
A Warrior Cry came out

New way of living
Came into view
New State of Being
Larger Awareness
Love emanating Outward

More birds started singing louder
New larger community
Symphonies of sounds
Filling regions of Earth
Healing, transforming, Awakening

~ Nancy Clark

Pierced My Heart

An arrow has pierced my heart
I will leave it in, for it comes from my Beloved

Everyone wants to remove the arrow
No! I am blessed with the pains of love

I see the world differently now,
my heart is yearning and aches for you

Passions for the Beloved
has caused my head to become dizzy

Worldly people don't understand
this kind of love and devotion

To lose oneself to the point
where you no longer exist

The Divine has pierced my heart,
no longer will live apart.

~ Nancy Clark

Our Time

A gentle touch
A loving word
"You'll just know"
Are the words I've heard.

That warm the heart,
Complete the soul.
I've come to you,
to make you whole.

You lived lifetimes
Of hit and miss.
Your prayers sing out,
for a love like this.

And when God's will
Is said and done.
After the heartache
Life's pain has run.

There'll be that season,
A time that's true.
I'll spend forever
Completing you.

~ Nancy Clark

Awake!

There is no life
Outside the Divine

Why are you claiming there is?

All that you see
is mind's illusion

Draw the true conclusion

You have played down
here so long
you have forgotten

Soaked with mind
bathed in time
played so long
you've grown tired
of the fire, that feeds you
pain and pleasure

Divine love
Wakes you up
From the dream

Awake!
Love has come
to take you Home

~ Nancy Clark

Beloved is Waiting

Why do you spend so much time on this side of heaven?
Infinite Presence is waiting for you to come up and experience
Oneness

There is a love so infinite and powerful,
waiting for you on the other side of the veil.

Treasures waiting for you to receive,
the veil is not that thick.

The Divine whispers, "Come and be with me my darling
Spend your moments with me forever
Let us become One"

Come to the place where the stars dance
Vistas on the other side are magnificent
Splendor, grandeur, majesty is some of the descriptions

You have to see for yourself
Come up to the place where I am waiting to receive you

The Secrets of the Universe are here to be discovered in the treasure chest.
Only through sincere love and devotion is the path revealed.

Only your love will carry you Home

~ Nancy Clark

Captivity

Born into Captivity, in the lower worlds
My soul is bound by duality, ever so tightly.

Inner and Outer storms, caused such heartache
Never understood, until one day.

Master Mystical Teacher entered my life
Explained desperate situation, Captivity.

As realization sunk in, a flood of my eyes
Pains of separation, longing to be free.

Born into Captivity
I have forgotten. What is freedom?

Freedom to be at home, in supreme abode
Only by Grace of Mystical Teacher, opportunity offered.

Have intense Love, spiritual practices, yearning,
daily downloads, Truth is my companion now.

Living behind bars, far away from home,
distraught with anguish, feeling so alone.

A True Teacher, showered mercy
Journey begins, homeward bound, Freedom!

~ Nancy Clark

Crazy Love

A long-time love has waited for you.
Infinite Presence has a Crazy Love just for you.
Always after your attention, your Soul.
Awaiting your love in return.
How long must you wait?

When will you see the falsehood in illusion?
Come to the Third Eye and be Loved.
I look, watch, and wait.
Hoping for a loving gaze my way.

Distractions everywhere
Outward movement
Further away from the Divine.
A deep mourning for your condition

You love the Un-real more than the Real.
You dance with Duality enjoying the whispers.

The Divine stands next to you seeing with heartache
Heartache, as you ignore the sweet kisses on your forehead.

This love is Real, Liberating, and Eternal.

~ Nancy Clark

Divine Love Call

If you only knew, the love for you

Stars would fall from the sky
just to show, how special you are

Laughter would grace you
Love would embrace you

Can you hear the sweet melody?
Soul always yearns for more

Life is simple, oh so sweet
one day, we will meet

Higher planes are ready
this Divine Union awaits
through Third Eye gate

Can you hear me whispering to you?

Think of me, talk with me
Constant love and conversation
this is possible, to have daily bliss
you never knew, it could be like this
a love call, to come Home

Time to leave, playground of illusion

Do you realize what awaits you?

If you really knew, how much you are loved
come, let's live in the higher realms together.

~ Nancy Clark

Grace

Grace has come
Showing the way

Grace promises
Safe journey home

Miracle of love
Grace from above

Diamonds mean nothing
when Love is near
Everything becomes
perfectly clear

Free flowing water
drink from the spring

Divine elixir
perfect fixer
for conclusion
of illusion

Drink up Grace
in thy place
of loneliness
and empty space

~ Nancy Clark

Heart Sense

My soul mate has arrived
Who fills me, deep inside
Each night going to sleep
Sweet dreams come complete

There is a warmth in my heart
And it does not end, we never part
The love I share is deep and true
I will love you forever, my promise to you

Life is precious and so sweet
The Divine whispered, today we meet
Life begins, side by side
Completing me, deep inside

A look to the future is bright and with cheer
The love of my life is now right here
Your eyes are beautiful to see
They have completely enraptured me

~ Nancy Clark

Drowning

Drowning in love
is scary, suffocating, risky

Love brings you closer, to the ocean.
Willing to dive in, the deep waters?

There is no bottom, to the ocean of love.
Powerful waves, will carry you away.

Love Waves are crashing,
onto the shore, touching your feet.

Ocean spray touches your lips,
I crave salty snacks!

Okay, I'll take a swim today
Ocean wraps all around
Love overwhelms me

Flipping over onto my back
the ocean carries me out
to deep waters

growing tired of fighting
this ride of life
sinking slowly
into this enrapture.

This drop becomes
one with the ocean.

~ Nancy Clark

Life Changes

Life changes, like the color of the leaves

Life changes, upon meeting The Divine

Water from the stream, now flows upwards

Animals look at you differently

Vibrations emanating from you, are higher

People feel your energy, more

Divine speaks with you softly, to prepare you, for your journey home

Let go, all is well, we are together now, never will part again

Sky is more a veil, you see deeper

Flowers dance, when the wind blows

People see how you, have changed

The circus of life loses its luster

Love beams brighter, than ever before

All-consuming love, to be in union with, The Presence

Life changes, upon meeting a Mystical Teacher

~ Nancy Clark

Love Call

Why does one cry, when they are in love?

They long to be with their lover

Think of the Beloved constantly

This deep love is not easy

The Soul cries for more

The body separates the two

Drop the silken robe of the body

Ego dies in order to awaken

Ego separates the two

Love comes rushing in

Causing the ego to die

A little more each day

You speak to me in poetry

A love call, to each Soul to come Home

~ Nancy Clark

Love Has Come

Love has come,
settling down,
into all the cells,
the body feels this kind of love,
is very unique and powerful.

Love is cleansing,
a calling come Home,
can't you hear the Sound,
of The Divine's Voice?

Love has come,
calling you back home,
remember me, remember me,
come home, focus homebound.

~ *Nancy Clark*

Forever Together

The clouds dance
Flowers smile
Stars twinkle brighter
What has caused this change?

Trees bend in the breeze
Birds sing then fly away
Gentle whispers to the Soul
The Divine is here to stay

Love has come
To be in love
With the Infinite Essence
Captivation with the Divine

A higher calling
A higher journey
A higher surrender
A higher Love

~ Nancy Clark

Love Rays

Radiating Love
Feeling the heat
Intensity of fire
Purification in process

Cleansing the temple
Freeing the Soul
Soaking up
Love Rays

Raising the temperature
Passions melt away
Love Powerful Rays
Burns away the pain

Dance in the sun
Absorption of the rays
Bask in the shower of
Divine's Grace

~ Nancy Clark

Endnotes

1. David Elkington, *The Ancient Language of Sacred Sound* (Rochester, VT: Inner Traditions, 2021), 93.
2. David Tame, *The Secret Power of Music: The Transformation of Self and Society through Musical Energy* (Rochester, VT: Destiny Books, 1984), 221.
3. Chuang Tzu, *Taoism*, 22 in International Religious Foundation, World Scripture: *A Comparative Anthology of Sacred Texts* (St. Paul, MN: Paragon House Publishers, 1995), 64.
4. Alistair Conwell, 160, *The Audible Life Stream: Ancient Secret of Dying while Living* (Winchester, UK: O-Books, 2010), 160.
5. Karen Kingston, *Creating Sacred Space with Feng Shui* (New York: Broadway Books, 1997), 163.
6. Joan Ranquet, *Energy Healing for Animals* (Boulder, CO: Sounds True, 2015), 13.
7. Maulana Rumi, "Music Master" in *The Essential Rumi*, translated by Coleman Barks (New York: HarperCollins, 2004), 106.
8. Drunvalo Melchizedek, *The Ancient Secret of the Flower of Life*, Vol. 1 (Flagstaff, AZ: Light Technology Publishing, 1998), 44.
9. Tame, 225.
10. Hafiz, "Perfection" in *The Gift: Poems by Hafiz, the Great Sufi Master*, translated by Daniel Ladinsky (New York: Penguin, 1999), 16.
11. David R. Hawkins, *Power vs. Force* (Carlsbad, CA: Hay House, 1995), 376.

12 Don Miguel Ruiz Jr., *The Mastery of Self* (San Antonio, TX: Hierophant Publishing, 2016), 49.
13 Paul Leon Masters, *Master's Degree Modules*, Vol. 2 (Sedona, AZ: University of Sedona, 2016), 80.
14 David R. Hawkins, *The Eye of the I* (Sedona, AZ: Veritas Publishing, 2001), 27
15 International Religious Foundation, 48.
16 Tame, 205.
17 Delores Cannon, *The Convoluted Universe*, Vol. 3 (Huntsville, AR: Ozark Mountain Publishing, 2008), 316.
18 The Bible. *Bible Hub*, www.biblehub.com. Accessed Feb. 2, 2022. New International Version Web.
19 Tame, 216.
20 Conwell, 76–77.
21 Tame, 206.
22 Elkington, 249.
23 Conwell, 161.
24 Tame, 23.
25 Manly P. Hall, *The Sacred Magic of the Qabbalah* (Eastford, CT: Martino Publishing, 2013), 64.
26 Vishnu Purana, *Hinduism*, 1:22 in International Religious Foundation, 53.
27 Tame, 213.
28 Elkington, 309–310.
29 Hall, 20–21.
30 Richard Heath, *Sacred Geometry* (Rochester, VT: Inner Traditions, 2021), 206.
31 Elkington, 235.
32 Conwell, 65.
33 Tame, 211.
34 Heath, 255–256.

35 Elkington, 247.
36 Conwell, 53.
37 Elkington, 312.
38 Tame, 22.
39 Heath, 99.
40 Elkington, 330.
4141 Cannon, 676.
42 David R. Hawkins, *Letting Go: The Pathway of Surrender* (Carlsbad, CA: Hay House, 2012), 191–192.
43 Tame, 226.
44 Elkington, 331.
45 Lynne McTaggart, *The Field* (New York: HarperCollins, 2008), 39, 41, 44.
46 Hall, 17.
47 Cannon, 321.
48 McTaggart, 50–51.
49 Tame, 225.
50 Elkington, 115.
51 Hawkins, *Power vs. Force*, 390.
52 Cannon, 329–330.
53 Hawkins, *The Eye of the I*, 57.
54 Paul Leon Masters, *Master's Degree Modules*, Vol. 1 (Sedona, AZ: University of Sedona, 2016), 20.
55 Samuel Sagan, *Awakening the Third Eye*, 3rd edition (Ravendale, CA: Point Horizon Institute, 1992), 82.
56 Rumi, "Story Water" in *The Essential Rumi*, 172.
57 Hawkins, 67.
585Delores Cannon, *The Three Waves of Volunteers and the New Earth* (Huntsville, AR: Ozark Mountain Publishing, 2011), 9.
59 Cannon, *The Convoluted Universe*, 683.
60 Hawkins, 202.

61 Masters, 1:22.
626 The Bible. *Bible Hub*, www.biblehub.com. Accessed Feb. 3, 2022. New Heart English Bible Web.
63 Hawkins, *Power vs. Force*, 384.
64 The Bible. *Bible Hub*, www.biblehub.com. Accessed Feb. 28, 2022. New Living Translation Web.
65 Cannon, *The Three Waves of Volunteers*, 18.
66 Hawkins, *The Eye of the I*, 214.
67 Cannon, *The Convoluted Universe*, 677.
68 Cannon, 19.
69 Cannon, 20, 211.
70 Hawkins, *Letting Go*, 254, 255.
71 Ruiz, 31.
72 Rumi, "Nothing Happens without You" in *Love's Ripening: Rumi on the Heart's Journey*, translated by Kabir Helminski and Ahmad Rezwani (Boulder, CO: Shambhala, 2008), 83.
73 Cannon, 332.
74 Hawkins, *The Eye of the I*, 62.
75 Hawkins, *Letting Go*, 192.
76 Kingston, 12, 13.
77 Elkington, 332.
78 Tame, 207.
79 Tame, 218.
80 Tame, 219.
81 "All-Pervasive Reality" in *International Religious Foundation*, 60.
82 Delores Cannon, *Between Death and Life* (Huntsville, AR: Ozark Mountain Publishing, 2019), 107.
83 Kanetomo Yoshida, "An Outline of Shinto" in International Religious Foundation, 62.
84 William Buhlman, *Adventures in the Afterlife* (Millsboro, DE: Osprey Press, 2013), 152.

85 Conwell, 117.
86 Hawkins, *The Eye of the I*, 58.
87 Hawkins, 209.
88 Cannon, *The Convoluted Universe*, 320.
89 Cannon, 328.
90 Hawkins, *Power vs. Force*, 394.
91 David R. Hawkins, *Transcending the Levels of Consciousness: The Stairway to Enlightenment* (Carlsbad, CA: Hay House, 2006), 29.

About the Author

Nancy Clark, Ph.D., is a mystical researcher and spiritual teacher with a Ph.D. in Mystical Research. Dr. Nancy Clark is the author of several books including *Our Divinity Revealed*, *Master Plant Teachers*, *Ascendance*, and *Divine Essence of Love*. Nancy's work focuses on metaphysics, spirituality, and esoteric studies, making her a unique voice in her field. Dr. Nancy helps Souls gain wisdoms from questions that seem a mystery. Connect with a Doctorate-Level, Mystical Spiritual Teacher.

nancyclarkphd.com

nancyclarkphd.com

www.ingramcontent.com/pod-product-compliance
Lightning Source LLC
Chambersburg PA
CBHW051946290426
44110CB00015B/2131